AN INTRODUCTION TO THE CULTURE AND HISTORY OF

THE TEOCHEWS IN SINGAPORE

Tan Gia Lim

World Scientific

NEW JERSEY • LONDON • SINGAPORE • BEIJING • SHANGHAI • HONG KONG • TAIPEI • CHENNAI • TOKYO

Published by
World Scientific Publishing Co. Pte. Ltd.
5 Toh Tuck Link, Singapore 596224
USA office: 27 Warren Street, Suite 401-402, Hackensack, NJ 07601
UK office: 57 Shelton Street, Covent Garden, London WC2H 9HE

National Library Board, Singapore Cataloguing in Publication Data
Names: Tan, Gia Lim.
Title: An Introduction to the Culture and History of the Teochews in Singapore / Tan Gia Lim.
Description: Singapore : World Scientific, [2018]
Identifiers: OCN 1033694471 | 978-981-32-3935-7 (hardcover)
Subjects: LCSH: Teochew (Chinese people)--Singapore--History. | Teochew (Chinese people)--Singapore-- Social life and customs.
Classification: DDC 305.895105957--dc23

AN INTRODUCTION TO THE CULTURE AND HISTORY OF THE TEOCHEWS IN SINGAPORE

ISBN 978-981-3239-35-7

FRONT COVER: 六十年代的回顾 THE 60'S IN RETROSPECT (1981). Chua Mia Tee, *Oil on canvas*

Printed in Singapore

This book is dedicated with gratitude to my great-grandfather and the many Teochew pioneers who took that leap of faith to "*guê huêng*" to "Selat" (过番到实叻) in pursuit of better lives for themselves, their families in Chaozhou and eventually for us, the Teochews in Singapore

Contents

Forewords 7

Preface 10

ROOTS

Origin 14
- Historical Administration
- The Teochew Eight Districts
- Teochew Enthnicity

Language 26
- Phrases and Folk Rhymes
- Narrative Literature

Migration to Southeast Asia 32
- Chinese in Southeast Asia
- Teochews in Southeast Asia
- Teochew Red Bow Junks
- Opening of Shantou
- Coolie Trade

NEW HOME

Teochews in Singapore 44
- Teochew Enclaves in Singapore
- Boat Quay Vicinity
- "Sing Pa Sa" Ellenborough Market Vicinity
- River Valley Road, Hill Street, North Boat Quay
- Rural Settlements and the "Kangs"

Traditional Occupations and Trades 51
- Plantation
- Trade and Commerce
- Textile and Piece Goods
- Lighter-boat
- Charcoal and Firewood
- Ceramics Trade and Production
- Postal Service & Remittance
- Banking

Education 64
- Tuan Mong School and Ngee Ann Secondary
- Tertiary Education
- Female Education
- Other Schools

Teochew Organisations 70
- Wak Hai Cheng Bio
- Ban See Soon Kongsee
- Ngee Ann Kongsi
- Chui Huay Lim Club
- Locality and Kinship Clan Associations
- Teochew Poit Ip Huay Kuan
- Teochew Federation
- Trade and Cultural Associations
- Shantang
- Dejiao Hui

Activities 86
- Politics
- Commerce
- Visual Arts
- Philanthropy

CULTURE

Beliefs, Customs and Practices 100
- Ancestral Reverence
- Deity Worship
- Festivals
- Rites of Passage

Cuisine & Tea Culture 111
- Cuisine
- Tea Culture

Vernacular Architecture 120
- Topologies and Decorative Elements
- Four Grand Residences
- House of Tan Yeok Nee

Performing Arts 126
- Opera
- Puppetry
- Instrumental Music
- Folk Dance

Folk Crafts 140
- Ceramics
- Wood Carving
- Chaozhou Embroidery
- Chaozhou Drawnwork

Selection of Localised Words in Singapore Teochew Dialect 146

Teochew Affiliated Organizations 152

References 156

FOREWORD

This book modestly describes itself as an 'Introduction' but is in fact a treasure trove of information on the history and culture of the Teochews in Singapore. Singapore is a rich tapestry with many threads woven into it. Without the Teochew threads, Singapore will look different like a picture with a colour missing.

It has been estimated that there are as many Teochews living outside Mainland China as there are living in China. Even within China, the Teochews are everywhere often playing a role disproportionate to their numbers. They are bound by a strong self-identity, which sometimes is criticized as clannish-ness. But this sense of identity is also a deep source of strength which partly explains the relative success of Teochews wherever they live. Curiously, even when younger members outside China do not speak the dialect well, they know who they are and often declare their Teochew identity with a measure of pride.

Tan Gia Lim's book explaining Teochew history and culture in English makes a valuable contribution to the development of Teochew culture in Singapore as part of our living heritage. It will help many young Teochews understand their own heritage better and others to understand them. Reading it as a Teochew, I feel encouraged to add material because there are so many aspects which fascinate. For example, the contribution of Teochews to the life of Singapore's Catholic community is profound and has its roots in China. Perhaps it is right that the author should describe the book as an 'Introduction' because, like a good Teochew cold dish, it whets your appetite for much more.

George Yeo

FOREWORD

An Introduction to the Culture and History of the Teochews in Singapore, by Tan Gia Lim, is a book for every Singaporean Teochew, especially those who want to learn more about their Teochew roots. Being a Teochew myself, I am glad that I was invited to pen a foreword for this book. With this "commitment", I was compelled to sit down and read, and with every page turned, I find myself more appreciative of and fascinated by my own Teochew roots.

From history, culture, tradition to people, Ms Tan had meticulously assembled a wellspring of information on Teochews in Singapore. And to my pleasant surprise, I am happy to note that Ms Tan hails from the post-1965 generation. This initiative driven by Ms Tan should connect well with the younger readers, and better connect our younger Teochew readers with the dialect group.

In recent years, there have been a lot of discussions about identity, heritage and culture in Singapore. Many Singaporeans are seeking to learn more about our origins and trying to make sense of what bond us together as one. A lot of initiatives have also been undertaken by the public and private sectors, for example our clan associations, to promote our identity, heritage and culture. In this case, a respected Chinese community leader, Professor Phua Kok Khoo, lent his support to the publication of this book and demonstrated the community spirit and mutual support we have in our society.

An Introduction to the Culture and History of the Teochews in Singapore is an admirable and interesting book that provides good insights into our Teochew community. I hope it would inspire a deeper understanding of Teochews around us; inspire other dialect groups and communities to compile and record their own unique heritage and culture; and above all, inspire every Singaporean to celebrate the identity, heritage and culture that make Singapore what it is today.

Ng Chee Meng

Preface

As a Teochew growing up in modern Singapore, I had little exposure to the Teochew dialect and its culture. I uttered a few words of the dialect once a year, have no recollection of watching Teochew operas as a child and have never stepped into a Teochew clan association until recently. I was, however, aware that non-Teochews often describe the Teochews as "*iun siu*" (幼秀, cultured) and "*haun liêng*" (好脸, proud), which I attributed to the gentler tone of the Teochew dialect and the wealth of the Teochew community. It took a visit to my late great-grandfather's ancestral home in 2012 to open my eyes to the vast world of Teochew history and culture. I was amazed that despite China's 21st century economic boom and the Teochews' business success in nearby Shenzhen and Guangzhou, many parts of the Chaoshan region remained untouched by the effects of modern economy. Large swaths of residences built in the late Ming and Qing periods stand intact in village settlements, ancestral halls are regularly restored and updated, and the prefecture capital city of old Chaozhou appears to be preserved in a time capsule. It is as if the Teochews have protected their cultural homeland from the onslaught of external forces, very much like what they did in 1860 when they fiercely repelled European powers' attempt to establish a foothold in Chaozhou city. For the first time, I also learnt of a discipline known as Chaozhou Studies (潮学) in which academics and researchers (nearly all of Teochew ethnicity) passionately research, document and share the culture and history of the Teochews within and outside China. Many of their works serve as information sources for this book.

The Chaoshan region, or Chaozhou to the overseas Teochews, is surprisingly small in size. Of approximately 11,000 square kilometres, it is slightly more than half the size of the Johor state. Compared with many other Han Chinese sub-ethnic groups, the Teochews and their culture were relatively late in formation, blossoming from the mid-Ming period and blooming during the Qing period. But what a culture! Within the span of a few hundred years, the Teochews not only formed their own dialect, but also their own distinctive tea culture, cuisine, opera, puppetry, music, dance, literature, ceramics art, embroidery, carvings, architecture and even founded a unique religious institution.

As the Teochews ventured out of China in large numbers in the late 19th and early 20th century, they brought many cultural elements to their new homes. Making up 15% of the Singapore population, they played significant roles in economy and education, but it is their out-sized presence in politics, philanthropy, Chinese literature and the visual arts that stood out. Their passion for culture saw them not only as custodians of traditional Chinese art forms but also as pioneers in contemporary visual arts where they founded the first modern art academy in Singapore and led the way for the Nanyang School, Social Realism and Installation Art movements. It dawned upon me that the Teochews are proud of their ethnic identity not because of the community's economic success, but because of the deep-rooted pride they have in their rich and unique culture which is reflected in their achievements in so many cultural spheres. The Teochews are "*haun liêng*" simply because they see themselves as "*iun siu*" people.

This book is a compilation of a "born-again" Teochew's journey in discovering her roots and heritage. It is meant as an initiation guide for anyone interested in learning more about the Teochew culture beyond the spoken dialect and cuisine. It does not attempt to serve as a complete or authoratative guide to Teochew culture and history. That mammoth task will take years and volumes of work given the breath and depth of the subject, as demonstrated by the tireless effort of academics and researchers involved in Chaozhou Studies. Some aspects left out in this book include Teochew secret society history, the Singapore Teochew Catholic community, Teochew writers' contribution to Singapore Chinese literature as well as Teochew culture elements not commonly known to Singapore Teochews, and there remains more research to be done on the origin of the Teochews in both Singapore and China. It is my wish that this rudimentary book would pique sufficient interest among readers to move them toward exploring more of the Teochew heritage and one day be active participants in the research and preservation of the culture.

Finally, the book is dedicated with gratitude to my late great-grandfather and the many Teochew pioneers who took that leap of faith to "*guê huêng*" to "Selat" (过番到实叻) in pursuit of better lives for themselves, their families in Chaozhou and eventually for us, the Teochews in Singapore.

Tan Gia Lim

ROOTS

ORIGIN

The term "Teochew" as it is used in Singapore and many other places around the world takes on several different meanings. Simply put, it is an English-language romanisation of the Chinese characters 潮州 as pronounced in the Teochew or Chaozhou dialect, a term which first entered historical records in AD 591 as the name of a prefecture in southern China. Other variant spellings include "Tiochiu" and "Teochiu" (also in the Teochew dialect), "Chiu Chow" in the Cantonese dialect, and of course, "Chaozhou" in Mandarin or hanyu pinyin.

"Teochew" also refers to the Chinese people who trace their ancestry to the Teochew prefecture and the same term is again used for the Chinese dialect spoken by this group of people. In other words, the term "Teochew" is used as a geographical, ethnic and linguistic term depending on the context. The Chinese language, however, establishes clearer distinctions. People who are "*diê ziu nang*" (潮州人, Teochews) speak "*diê ziu uê*" (潮州话, Teochew dialect) and they share an ancestry and culture linked to a former prefecture known as "*diê ziu hu*" (潮州府, Chaozhoufu) or "*diê ziu*" (潮州, Chaozhou) located within the Guangdong province.

Chaozhou was one of the several prefectures that made up the Guangdong province in imperial China and shared a border with Fujian province on to the northeast. Within the old Chaozhou prefecture were also several counties such as Chenghai (澄海) and Jieyang (揭阳), and most Teochews around the world can trace their ancestry to the villages or towns located in these counties. After the opening of the Shantou (汕头) port to foreign trade in 1860, many Teochews in search of a better living left their villages for Shantou (then located within Chenghai county) where they boarded vessels to take them to various locations in Southeast Asia or what was then known as Nanyang, with the majority settling in Siam, the Dutch East Indies, British Malaya and Singapore.

While many overseas Teochews continue to refer to this land of their ancestry as Chaozhou, it is known in China today as the Chaoshan region (潮汕地区), or more specifically, the "Three Cities of the Chaoshan region" (潮汕三市), comprising Shantou, Chaozhou and Jieyang. The term "Chaoshan", coined by taking the first characters of the names Chaozhou and Shantou and joining them together, was first publicly known via the name of the Chao Chow and Swatow Railway Company (潮汕铁路有限公司) of 1904 which was set up to build and run the rail route between the historical city of Chaozhou and the port city of Shantou. It came into popular use as the Shantou port grew and overtook the old Chaozhou prefectural city as the major population centre of the entire Teochew dialect-speaking region in China during the first half of the 20th century. With the elevation of the former Jieyang county to the status of city and putting it on par with Shantou and Chaozhou in 1991, the region began to be collectively referred to as the "Three Cities of the Chaoshan region", but still "Chaoshan" in short. Essentially retaining the geographical boundaries of the now-defunct Chaozhou prefecture, their populations share a common culture known as Chaoshan culture. At the end of 2010, the total permanent population of the three cities stood at 15,037,945. One estimate puts the population of overseas Teochews to be equivalent to that number.

Located in eastern Guangdong with latitude spanning 22°53' to 24°14'N and longitude 115°20' to 117°20'E, the Chaoshan region is 10,451 sq km in size, of which approximately one third or 3,207 sq km consists of flatland. It has a subtropical climate where winters are short and mild and summers are long and humid. Annual rainfall ranges from 1300 to 2200 mm and occurs mostly between April to September and the region is subjected to tropical typhoons in summer. The Chaoshan region faces the South China Sea with a long coastline of 325.6 km that is dotted with bays, inlets and islands, the largest island being Nan'ao Island.

Described as "high on the northwest and low at the southeast" the region's physical landscape is defined by two mountain ranges and three inland rivers. Its backbone is made up of highlands on the west, the most notable being the Fenghuangshan (凤凰山, Phoenix Mountain Range) and the Lianhuashan (莲花山, Lotus Mountain Range). Lianhuashan separates the region from the predominantly Cantonese-speaking Pearl Delta region in the west while Fenghuangshan forms a natural boundary to the Hakka-speaking region in the north. Chaoshan region's flatland terrain is served by three major rivers and their tributaries: the Hanjiang (韩江, Han River), the Rongjiang (榕江, Rong River) and the Lianjiang (练江, Lian River). The Hanjiang, which flows through Chaozhou city to Shantou city before pouring into the South China Sea, forms the vital Hanjiang Delta (韩江三角洲, Han River Delta) where the largest concentration of settlements are located.

The Chaoshan region is bordered by the Hokkien-speaking Zhangzhou (漳州) to its east and northeast, the Hakka-speaking Meizhou (梅州) in the northwest and the South China Sea in the southeast. This simultaneously open and enclosed terrain allows the region to absorb and integrate external cultural influences and yet is self-contained enough to cultivate its own unique cultural identity. Although historically governed as part of Guangdong province, the Chaoshan region's distance from the Cantonese culture hub of Guangzhou meant lesser interaction with the Cantonese people, resulting in reduced similarities between the Cantonese and Teochew cultures. Instead, closer proximity and the lack of geographical barriers between the Chaoshan region and southern Fujian province allowed for the people of both areas to interact easily, resulting in the closeness of Chaoshan culture with southern Fujian or Southern Min (闽南) culture — commonly known as Hokkien culture in Singapore and Malaysia.

Historical Administration

When the first Chinese Emperor, Qin Shihuang, established the Qin dynasty (221 - 206 BC) to rule over China, he set up an administrative system governed on two levels, commanderies (郡) and counties (县). In 214 BC three commanderies — Xiangjun (象郡), Guilin (桂林) and Nanhai (南海) — were established in southern China. Sometime between the end of the Qin dynasty and the beginning of the Han dynasty, a Qin official Zhao Tuo (赵佗) established the Nanyue Kingdom (南越国) which ruled over a large swath of southern China and a Jieyang county (揭阳县) was believed to be first established during this Nanyue Kingdom period. This was the very first time a locale name of Chaozhou was mentioned in official Chinese history, although historians remain unclear as to the exact location of this first Jieyang or whether it shared the same geographical boundaries as its present-day namesake. In 111 BC, Emperor Han Wudi of the Han dynasty (206 BC – AD 220) conquered the region and brought the Nanyue Kingdom under Han rule. He then went about enlarging the Nanhai commandery to administer the six counties of Panyu (番禺), Boluo (博罗), Zhongsu (中宿), Longchuan (龙川), Sihui (四会) and Jieyang (揭阳).

Map of Guangdong province and its prefectures during the Qing dynasty. The four major dialect groups in the Guangzhou province are the Cantonese, Hainanese, Hakkas and Teochews. Chaozhou prefecture, where the Teochews hailed from, is located at the eastern end of the province and shares a border with Fujian province.

During the Eastern Jin dynasty (AD 317 - 420), a three-tier administrative system consisting of prefecture, commandery and county was adopted. In AD 413, the Yi'an commandery (义安郡) was established in what is today the Chaoshan region. Governed by Guangzhou prefecture (广州) and with five counties under its jurisdiction - namely Haiyang (海阳), which doubled as its capital, Sui'an (绥安), Haining (海宁), Chaoyang (潮阳) and Yizhao (义招), the term Yi'an would be source of inspiration for Singapore Teochew pioneer Seah Eu Chin when he named the organisation he founded in 1845 the Ngee Ann Kongsi, Ngee Ann being the Teochew dialect rendition of the term Yi'an.

The Sui dynasty (AD 581 – 618) abolished the commandery but retained the prefecture - which it called *zhou* (州) – as well as the county, and in AD 591, the region comprising of what was formerly the Yi'an commandery was renamed Chaozhou (潮州) or "Tidal Prefecture", named after the flowing *chao* (潮, tides) of the waters surrounding the prefecture (在潮之洲，潮水往复). This would be the first time the name Chaozhou came into being, albeit for a short period, as it reverted to Yi'an in AD 607 when the Sui government restored the commandery system.

The name Chaozhou was revived in AD 622 during the reign of Tang Emperor Gaozu, only to be dropped in favour of Chaoyang commandery (潮阳郡) in AD 742, before finally reverting to Chaozhou in AD 758. From this point onwards, the name Chaozhou would be used throughout Chinese history.

Chaozhou retained its name throughout the rest of the Tang dynasty and the entire Song dynasty (960 – 1279). During the Yuan dynasty (1271 – 1368), Chaozhou became known as Chaozhoudao (潮州道) when the Mongol government decided to use the term *dao* (道) to name its prefectures. Dao was changed to *fu* (府) in the Ming dynasty (1368 – 1644), resulting in the name Chaozhoufu (潮州府), a name which was retained during the Qing dynasty (1644 – 1911).

By 1634, Chaozhoufu administered a total of eleven counties: Haiyang (海阳), Chaoyang (潮阳), Jieyang (揭阳), Raoping (饶平), Huilai (惠来), Chenghai (澄海), Puning (普宁), Pingyuan (平远), Chenxiang (程乡), Dabu (大埔) and Zhengping (镇平), the largest number of counties in the history of Chaozhou. In 1733, Pingyuan (平远), Chenxiang (程乡) and Zhengping (镇平) were merged into a new prefecture Jiayingzhou (嘉应州). The geographical boundaries of Chaozhou as we know it today came into being around 1738 when Fengshun (丰顺) was added to the remaining eight counties administrated under the Chaozhou prefecture, namely Haiyang (海阳), Chaoyang (潮阳), Jieyang (揭阳), Raoping (饶平), Huilai (惠来), Chenghai (澄海), Puning (普宁) as well as Dabu (大埔). This composition of nine counties in Chaozhou would remain throughout the Qing dynasty until the establishment of the Republic in 1912.

The Republic period (1912 – 1949) saw numerous changes to the administrative structure of the Chaoshan region. Nan'ao was established as a county in 1912 and Haiyang was renamed Chao'an in 1914. Shantou, which opened as a port city in 1860, was separated from Chenghai county in 1921 and elevated to the status of a city in 1930. From then on, the term "Chaoshan" began to gain prominence.

After the formation of the People's Republic of China in 1949, the Chaoshan Zone (潮汕专区) was established in 1950 with one city, Shantou, and eight counties: Chao'an (潮安), Chaoyang (潮阳), Jieyang (揭阳), Raoping (饶平), Huilai (惠来), Chenghai (澄海), Puning (普宁) and Nan'ao (南澳). There were other changes from 1950 to 1983 when the Chaoshan region and combination of other nearby counties formed the Yuedong Administrative Zone (粤东行政区) and Shantou Region (汕头地区). In December 1983, the Shantou Region was replaced by the Shantou administrative city (汕头市) which managed the eight counties and one city. A final redrawing and restructuring of the Chaoshan region took place in November 1991 which saw Shantou city divided into three prefectural-level cities (地级市): Shantou, Chaozhou and Jieyang. These three cities became collectively referred to as the "Three cities of the Chaoshan region" (潮汕三市), or "Chaoshan" in short. The region has a combined population of 15,037,945 (2010 figures) covering a land area of some 10,451 sq km in size. As of 2014, the three cities oversaw jurisdiction over the following areas:

the 1930s, Father Maglioni, an Italian missionary, was the first to discover traces of Neolithic culture in the Lufeng (陆丰) region. In the 1950s, Chinese archaeologists also uncovered major Neolithic sites within the Chaoshan region, the most significant being the ones at Chenqiaocun (陈桥村) and Shiweishan (石尾山) in Chao'an county. The primitive pottery found at the Chenqiaocun site included some coarse sand-tempered pots decorated with incised patterns in the neck and shoulder area.

In 1974, Chinese archaeologists uncovered more than 300 late Neolithic artefacts consisting of mainly stone tools and pottery wares from 21 sites within the vicinity of Fubin, Raoping. Amongst these artefacts was a bronze dagger-axe (戈) with some characteristics associated with the late Shang period. Similar discoveries of late Neolithic artefacts with traces of Bronze Age wares in other sites led scholars in the 1990s to use the term "Fubin Culture" (浮滨文化) to describe this late Neolithic/early Bronze Age civilization located in eastern Guangdong province and southern Fujian province 2,800 to 3,500 years ago. The transition from the Neolithic Age to the Bronze Age was slower in the south compared to the central plains of northern China and there is insufficient evidence to support the presence of any state or kingdom, although a tribal form of government is possible.

During the Warring States period in China, the State of Chu defeated the State of Yue and some Yue people moved south. Over the next few centuries, the Yue people would displace the Fubin Culture and become the dominant cultural influence in southern China, producing what is known today as the Southern Yue culture (南越文化), as evidenced by the discovery of bronze weapons and pottery with Yue culture symbols in modern Jieyang and Jiexi areas.

In 204 BC, soon after the collapse of the Qin empire, a Qin military officer Zhao Tuo (赵佗) founded the Southern Yue or Nanyue Kingdom (南越国) with its capital in Panyu in modern-day Guangdong province. Zhaotuo adopted the local Southern Yue culture while implementing the Qin commandery-county administrative structures. The Nanyue Kingdom fell in 111 BC after it was conquered by Emperor Wu Di of the Han dynasty and the whole of south-eastern China, including modern-day Chaoshan region, came directly under central government rule, laying the foundation for the spread of Han Chinese civilisation into the region. Yet despite increased interaction between northern and southern China, full-scale sinicisation of the Chaoshan region remained slow and limited compared with the Pearl River Delta region located further south.

Undated photo of She natives (畲族) at work. The natives of the Chaoshan region comprised two main groups: the *Liao* people (僚人) and the *Li* people (俚人). The Liao people mostly lived on the Guangdong-Fujian-Jiangxi borders and were the ancestors of the She and *Dan* (蛋族). They kept a distance from the Han Chinese immigrants and were often engaged in confrontation with the latter group. The Li people lived on the plains of southern China and they were the ancestors of present day Zhuang people (壮族). They adopted Han culture at an early stage and a number of their tribe leaders were Han Chinese. The Li people were militarily powerful and played vital roles in the political stability of the region during the Sui and Tang periods.

The "Yongjia Disturbance" (永嘉之乱) in the early 4th century – in which Xiongnu nomads from the north attacked Luoyang, the capital of the Western Jin dynasty – and the subsequent political unrest in the region resulted in the first mass movement of ethnic Han Chinese nobility class and their culture from north to south China, known in history as the "Southward Movement of Han Civilisation" (衣冠南渡). Members of the Jin imperial family and court officials who fled south helped established the Eastern Jin dynasty (AD 317 – 420) with its capital in modern day Nanjing. During the Eastern Jin period, the need to provide direct administration over a growing population in the Chaoshan region due to the influx of Han Chinese saw the establishment of the Yi'an commandery in AD 413. Nevertheless, these Han Chinese immigrants and the natives of the Chaoshan region would continue to remain culturally distinct from one another.

Further population growth in the Chaoshan region during the Sui period (AD 589 – 618) saw its status elevated to that of a prefecture (州) in the year AD 591 and the debut of the name Chaozhou (潮州) - or "*diê ziu*" as pronounced in the Teochew dialect, "Chao" meaning "tide" and referring to the tides or waves that lapped at the region's coastlines. Han Chinese political and cultural influence increased during the Tang period (AD 618 – 907) after the Tang General *Chen Zheng* (陈政) and his descendants helped suppress a series of rebellions in southern China and brought the region under Tang rule. The uprisings, staged mainly by natives in Chaozhou and Quanzhou in neighbouring Fujian province and took place over a period of nearly 50 years from AD 669 to 715, were put down by first Chen Zheng, then his son *Chen Yuanguang* (陈元光) and finally his grandson *Chen Xiang* (陈向) with the help of other northern migrants, resulting in a further consolidation of Han Chinese culture in the conquered territories.

Chaozhou's distance from the Tang capital of Chang'an and its sparse population made it an ideal location to exile errant court officals as a form of punishment for offending the imperial order. During the Tang dynasty, a total of twelve officials were exiled to Chaozhou, the most prominent being a member of the renowned Tang literati and Confucian scholar *Han Yu* (韩愈), who was sent to Chaozhou in AD 819 for daring to criticise the Tang Emperor's devotion to a bone-relic said to be that of Buddha's. By the end of the Tang dynasty in AD 901, the population of Chaozhou had grown to nearly 80,000 people, up from 37,000 at the beginning of the dynasty in AD 618.

Han Yu (韩愈) promoted education and carried out a series of reforms like the abolishment of slavery, and was even said to have helped rid the main river in Chaozhou of crocodiles during his period of exile in the city. He was credited for the spread of sinification and literacy in Chaozhou and later generations honoured him by naming the main waterway and the hill overlooking the city from across the river Hanjiang (韩江) and Hanshan (韩山) respectively.

Chaozhou culture, as we know it today, took root during the Song period (AD 960 - 1279) when large waves of immigrants from the Fujian province moved into the Chaoshan region, bringing along with them the Min (闽) culture, Min being the abbreviation for Fujian. This migrant culture from Fujian soon occupied mainstream position in the Chaoshan region, out of which eventually evolved the Chaozhou culture that one is familiar with today, with its strong Minnan or southern Fujian influence and close similarities in the areas of language, religious practices as well as culture and customs.

By the period of the Song dynasty (AD 960 - 1279), Fujian province had become a major economic and cultural centre in southern China, thanks to the huge influx of Han Chinese from northern and central China – the cradle of Chinese civilisation – who had been seeking refuge in the southern province starting from the Yongjia Disturbance in the 4th century. Over time, rapid population growth in Fujian province especially in Putian and Quanzhou put intense pressure on land that was available for economic activities and this in turn caused the people from these overcrowded regions to move further south into the relatively underpopulated Chaozhou.

Compared with past migrations, there was a larger degree of assimilation between the newcomers and the locals this time. This massive wave of migrants from neighbouring Fujian caused the population of Chaozhou to surge from 135,000 people in AD 976 to 612,000 people by the year 1246, with the total number of households

Table 1: Settlement Formation in Chaozhou

By Period	Song & earlier		Yuan		Ming		Qing		Total	
Jieyang (294 villages)	61	25.8%	30	12.7%	107	45.3%	38	16.1%	236	100.0%
Fuyangzhen, Chao'an (94 villages)	25	26.6%	7	7.4%	61	64.9%	1	1.1%	94	100.0%
Chenghai (311 villages)	76	24.4%	11	3.5%	116	37.3%	108	34.7%	311	100.0%

By Founders' Origin	Fujian		Local		Guangdong		Others		Unknown		Total	
Jieyang (294 villages)	100	42.4%	42	17.8%	0	0.0%	13	5.5%	81	34.3%	236	100%
Fuyangzhen, Chaoan (94 villages)	50	53.2%	21	22.3%	3	3.2%	0	0.0%	20	21.3%	94	100%

Source: Huang Ting, Du Jingguo (2001). *Chaoshan Shi Shang Ce*. China: Guangdong People's Publishing House

also going up from some 30,000 in 968 to around 135,000 households by 1236. Among those who migrated to Chaozhou during the Song period were many from the noble and official classes, and many Teochew clans today can trace their ancestry to these migrants from Fujian province.

During the Song period, many officials of Fujian descent appointed by the imperial court to govern Chaozhou were strong advocates of education. Through the establishment of schools and the provision of funds to help students in their educational pursuits, these officials made education more widespread and accessible in Chaozhou. Bearing testimony to the growth in sinification and literacy rate in Chaozhou is the fact that more than 10,000 people (or one in every 70 people) registered and sat for the imperial examinations in the year 1267 alone, up from 3,000 in 1174.

Save for the chaotic initial years and turbulent last days of the Yuan period (AD 1278 - 1368), Chaozhou remained relatively stable during the Mongol rule, with substantial economic and cultural progress. A study by a leading Chaozhou studies scholar Professor Huang Ting, placed the population of Chaozhou at between 580,000 to 633,000 in the year 1350.

The Chaozhou population grew rapidly during the Ming dynasty (AD 1368 - 1644) due to another large wave of migrants from Fujian province. According to a Qing period edition of "The Chaozhou Gazetteer" (潮州府志), the prefecture's registered population grew from 96,784 in 1391 to 540,850 in 1592, while another study by Professor Huang Ting estimated that the population in Chaozhou grew from some 428,000 people during the transition period between the Yuan and Ming periods, to peak at around 950,000 in the year 1551. The increase in population together with improved irrigation saw higher productivity in agriculture to the extent that Chaozhou was now able to produce excess food items for export. There were also other economic activities such as the production of salt, textile, and metal which led to the growth of trade with other parts of China and even outside of China despite the Ming ban on maritime commerce. With economic prosperity came the expansion of education and cultural development and it was during the Ming period that Chaozhou culture became distinct from Minnan culture. Many key elements of Chaozhou culture such as its dialect, opera, music and tea culture came into being during this period.

Chaozhou's population and economy grew further during the Qing period (1644 - 1912) especially after the Qing government cemented its control of China with the suppression of the Formosa rebellion in 1684. As the production of rice was no longer sufficient to feed the growing population in the Chaoshan region, Chaozhou traders were now permitted to travel to Siam to import rice. At the same time, growers in Chaozhou also intensified the cultivation of cash crops like sugar and cotton in order to achieve higher returns from the land. Trade became an important economic activities and Chaozhou merchants were found in many cities in China. Overseas emigration increased after the signing of the Treaty of Tien-tsin in 1858 following China's defeat in the Second Opium War – which opened up more ports in China including Shantou to foreign trade and also legalized Chinese emigration. Noteworthy is the fact that wealth from trade and money remitted by overseas Teochews actually helped fund the development of the Chaozhou culture, which was further refined during the Qing period into the form that all of us are familiar with today.

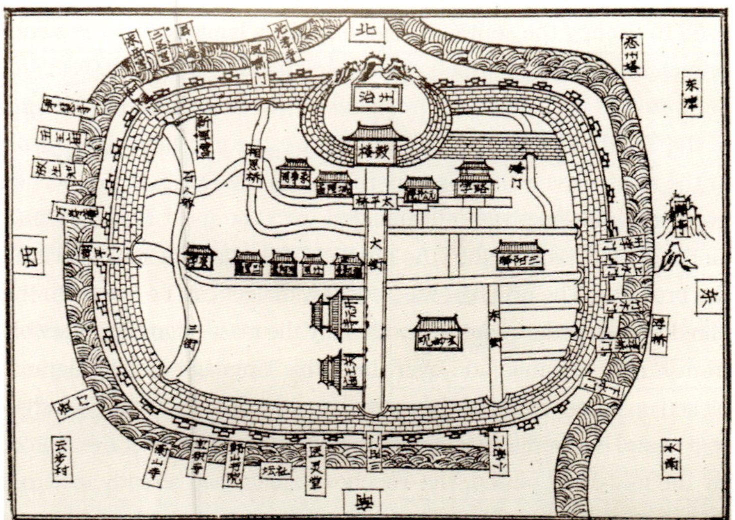

宋代潮州古城图（摘自明《永乐大典》卷5343）

Prefecture capital city of Chaozhou during the Song dynasty (960-1279) as illustrated in the Ming Encyclopedia Volume 5343. The development of Chaozhou culture and ethnicity took root during this period.

Ming painting of Longhu Guzai (龙湖古寨), a township located south of the prefecture capital city. The settlement came into being during the Song dynasty and prospered during the Ming dynasty as a trading centre. Such mature townships were not uncommon in Chaozhou during the Ming dynasty.

and 1433. Chinese merchants, especially those from the Fujian province, began to settle in greater numbers in Malacca until the Chinese settlement was large enough for the Portuguese to appoint a Kapitan in the 1560s. The Chinese' intermarriage with the locals gave rise to a new Chinese diaspora on the Malay peninsula known as the Baba Chinese.

Not long after the Dutch East India Company founded Batavia in 1619, Chinese merchants involved in the pepper trade from nearby Banten were encouraged to move in the new port settlement. Acting as contractors and tax farmers for the Dutch, they recruited labourers and craftsmen from China and also supplied the building materials for the construction of buildings and city walls

After the Spanish established control of Manila in 1571, Fujian merchants began a lucrative trade in exchanging Chinese goods such as textile, foodstuff, ironware and more for Philippines products and Mexican silver coins. By 1603, the Chinese population in Manila had grown to more than 20,000 to include various craftsmen in addition to merchants. Living in designated areas known as parians, Chinese who were of pure Chinese ancestry were termed as *sangley*, while the descendants of Chinese immigrants who married local women were known as *mestizo de sangley*.

Trade and other economic opportunities were the primary reasons that brought these early Chinese to Southeast Asia, or Nanyang as it was then called by the Chinese. Along the sea routes, ships would ride on the southwest monsoons from December to March to sail to Southeast Asia, and would then use the northeast monsoons from June to September to travel back to China. In between the two monsoon seasons, Chinese sailing ships and their crew would remain in Southeast Asia and some of them would even choose to settle down in the region for a longer period. The Chinese invention of the compass during the Song dynasty was a technological breakthrough that helped boost navigational accuracy. All in all, official encouragement of maritime trade during the Song and Yuan dynasties as well as overall improvements in shipbuilding and navigational technologies greatly increased commerce between China and Southeast Asia. However, this early movement of Chinese pales in comparison to the large scale migration from the various treaty ports in the 19th and 20th century.

By the mid-19th century, European powers had established a number of colonies in Southeast Asia and these thriving colonies created a demand for labour to work on infrastructure and in the various plantations and mines. The British implementation of the Residency system created order in the tin mining areas of peninsula Malaya, and soaring tin production led to an influx of Chinese labour who arrived at an annual rate of 100,000 throughout most of the period 1892-1932.

The Qing government initially imposed restrictions on Chinese migration overseas, though an imperial decree in 1754 legalized multiple departures and returns of bona fide traders to Southeast Asia but sojourning labourers were not mentioned. These restrictions were gradually relaxed starting with the Treaty of Tientsin and by 1893 the ban was lifted, opening the floodgate for Chinese overseas migration. After European powers forced the Qing government to sign a number of "unequal treaties" at the end of two Opium Wars, treaty ports like Xiamen and Shantou opened to European trading ships. The arrival of European steamships at these ports meant that people could travel in larger numbers and with greater frequency compared to sailing ships dependent on the seasonal winds.

In a 1934 study on the reasons for migration conducted on 905 Nanyang Chinese immigrants by the Chinese sociologist Ch'en Ta (陈达), it was revealed that 69.95% immigrated due to economic pressure, 19.45% due to connections in Nanyang, with the rest citing natural disasters, job opportunities and other factors. These factors differ from the mainly trade and political factors accounting for the early movement of Chinese to Southeast Asia.

Teochews in Southeast Asia

Hailing from a region with a long coastline meant that the Chaozhou people had a natural affinity with the seas and indeed they were engaged in seafaring activities from very early times. Since the Tang dynasty, foreign ships were known to dock and trade in ports near the

Chaoshan region. These maritime activities would intensify during the Song and Yuan periods, as evinced by the discovery of fragments of Song ceramics produced by Chaozhou's Bijiashan (笔架山) kilns in many parts of Southeast Asia and beyond.

During the Ming period, save for the reigns of Emperor Yongle (1402 – 1424) and Emperor Xuande (1425 – 1435) in which Admiral Cheng Ho undertook his historic sea expeditions, subsequent Ming emperors mostly imposed a ban on non-official maritime activities, including trade in an attempt to curb piracy and civil disobedience.

Yet the ban proved ineffective in Chaozhou and illegal trade continued with ports in Zhelin (柘林) of Raoping and on the island of Nan'ao (南澳) becoming centres of activity for both local and foreign traders from Japan and Siam. The reigns of Emperor Jiajing (1522 - 1566) and Emperor Wanli (1566 – 1572) saw a period of intense confrontation between the imperial court and these illegal Teochew traders who were mostly armed to fend off the government. To escape government persecution, some of these Teochew smugglers like *Lin Feng* (林凤) and *Lin Daoqian* (林道乾) fled with thousands of their followers to Luzon and Patani respectively, setting the precedent for migration to Southeast Asia by Teochews. *Zhang Lian* (张琏) of Raoping waged a three-year-long battle with Emperor Jiajing's forces before escaping to Nanyang and was reportedly sighted with his followers in Palembang in 1577.

The maritime ban continued into the early years of the Qing dynasty and was even tightened in Chaozhou to contain local support for the anti-Manchu rebellion movement. These restrictions were only lifted in 1684 after the rebel forces in neighbouring Formosa (current Taiwan) were finally quashed. The peace and stability that followed resulted in rapid population growth, putting increasing strain on food production in the country. To alleviate the rice shortage in China, rice import from Siam was eventually allowed by the Qing government, especially during the reigns of Emperor Yongzheng (1722 –1735) and Emperor Qianlong (1735 – 1796), and no duties were imposed on the imported rice.

Ports such as Zhanglin (樟林) in Chenghai and Anbu (庵埠) in Haiyang (later renamed Chao'an) rose to prominence, with Zhanglin becoming the centre of the rice trade with Siam. The rice trade expanded the sea trade routes and the Zhanglin-Siam connection facilitated the migration of Teochews to Siam in large numbers. This was the first wave of Teochew migration to Southeast Asia with Siam as a major destination for these Teochew migrants as Siam offered abundant opportunities in agriculture and trade for the newcomers. As their numbers grew, some of these Teochew immigrants and their descendants even made forays into local politics, as was the case of King Taksin (郑信), the son of a Teochew immigrant from Chenghai who founded the Thonburi dynasty and ruled Siam from 1767 to 1782 before he was overthrown. Today, Teochews make up the largest share of the Chinese in Thailand, especially in Bangkok.

Teochew migration to the Dutch East Indies also took place around the 1700s. Records and artefacts show that the Teochews were planting and trading in gambier in the Riau islands as early as the 18th century before they moved to Singapore. As was with the case of Siam's King Taksin, a certain *Zhang Jiezhu* (张杰诸) from Chaozhou is also believed to have established a kingdom in Ampenan, Lombok sometime during the 19th century before his wealth and territory were seized by the Dutch in 1882. Meanwhile, historical records of the Hakka-based Lanfang Kongsi in West Kalimantan also noted the presence of immigrants from Chaoyang and Jieyang involved in gold mining activities in the Mandor region in western Borneo.

The opening of Shantou as a treaty port in 1860 and the arrival of steamships ushered in the age of massive overseas Teochew migration. Many Teochews, faced with poor economic conditions as well as political instability and social unrest in their hometowns, took the opportunity to "*guê huêng*" (过番), i.e. to seek their fortune in foreign lands.

The movement of people from Shantou to Southeast Asia and other parts of the world between 1860 and the establishment of the Republic of China in 1912, constituted part of the second wave of total Chinese migration overseas. Between 1869 and 1911, the net number of people departing from Shantou for the Straits Settlements, Bangkok, Saigon and Sumatra was 1.9 million with the Straits Settlements having attracting the highest number at 1.3 million. The end of World War II saw Shantou regaining its role as the busiest port of embarkment for overseas Chinese migration. Migration to Nanyang in 1946, 1947 and 1948 were 48,228, 30,501 (6 months) and 57,628 (11 months) respectively.

People who "*guê huêng*" (过番) were termed as "*huêng kêh*" (番客) and to many early Teochew immigrants, Singapore was also known as "*sig lag bo*" (实叻坡). Even today, many older Teochews still use the phrase "*guê huêng gau sig la* " (过番到实叻) to refer to their migration journey from Chaozhou to Singapore.

Teochew Red Bow Junks

The shipping vessels that brought goods and Teochew immigrants to Selat in early 19th century were sturdy wooden sailing ships with bright red bows and big eyes painted on the sides, known as "*ang tau zung*" (红头船, red bow junks). After lifting the maritime ban for civilian vessels, the Qing government mandated that the bows of civilian ships from each province be painted in different colours to make visual inspection at sea easier: Guangdong province (which Chaozhou is under) red, Fujian province green, Zhejiang province white and Jiangsu province black. The Teochews named their ships "*ang tau zung*" and painted eyes on the side of the boats as this supposedly helped the ships to "see" and not lose their way on their journeys. The "*ang tau zung*" came into prominence as a result of the Siam rice trade where Teochew merchants made their way to Siam to import rice into China. Zhanglin (樟林) in Chenghai, a key port for the rice trade, became known as the "Hometown of the Red Bow Junks". Many of the ships used by the Teochews were made in Bangkok due to the availability of wood and lower cost of production. The other "*ang tau zing*" ports in Chaozhou were Anbu (庵埠), Zhelin (柘林) and Shantou (汕头). From Chaozhou, these merchant vessels sailed northwards to Shanghai, Tianjin and Qingdao and southwards to Guangzhou, Hainan, Siam and other parts of Southeast Asia.

Capable of carrying loads of up till to 300 tons, these ships were dependent on the monsoon winds for the voyage to and from China and hence could only travel once a year. They would depart China for Southeast Asia with the northeast monsoon from December to March and return with the southwest monsoon which blows from June to September. The first "*ang tau zung*" arrived in Singapore shortly after the arrival of the first sail ship from Amoy in 1821. The ships started off primarily as merchant ships bringing goods such as ceramics and dried foodstuff from China and returning to China with opium, shark's fin and Straits products. It was later that more Teochew immigrants boarded the ships to come to Southeast Asia.

Because these junks could only make one return trip a year, the frequency of contact between Chaozhou and Southeast Asia was not high and the number of immigrants arriving by "*ang tau zung*" was small compared to those who would come later by steamships from Shantou. Even though it was the steamships which brought the majority of Teochews immigrants to their overseas destinations, the "*ang tau zung*" remains a strong symbol for the Teochew immigrants, representing their pioneering spirit and unyielding quest in seeking better lives for themselves in foreign lands.

Table 2: Red Bow Junks Arrivals in Singapore

	1849		1850		1851		1852	
	Ship	Passenger	Ship	Passenger	Ship	Passenger	Ship	Passenger
Chonglim	6	1,570	7	2,110	7	2,655	8	2,683
Swatow	2	250	2	600	2	370	3	1,000
Teochew	1	255	3	250	1	10	3	244
Total		2,075		2,960		3,035		3,927

Source: "Straits Time and The Singapore Free Press 1849-1852

In Singapore the "*ang tau zung*" is manifested in the goods-carrying bum boats or "twakows" plying the Singapore River from Boat Quay to Clarke Quay. Twakows owned by Hokkiens had bows coloured mainly in green and sometimes white, while the Teochew-owned retained their bright red bows.

Red bow junks at the Singapore waterfront (1848-49).

NEW HOME

Teochews in Singapore

The Teochews were known to reside on the Malay Peninsula and the Riau islands before the British arrived in Singapore. Wee Ah Heng, father of Wee Ah Hood, had relocated from Haiyang (later renamed Chao'an) county to Malacca by 1810 and owned a number of Chinese junks trading between Singapore and Selangor. Teochews were believed to have settled in the Riau islands by the 18th century and were engaged in the growing and trading of gambier.

When Raffles landed on Singapore in 1819,, there were already some Chinese gambier planters on the island, most of whom were Teochews who moved here from the Riau Islands. In William Farqhuar's report to Raffles in 1822, he mentioned that prior to the Singapore's founding, gambier plantations already existed around Government Hill (present day Fort Canning Hill). According to colonial government records, there was a sale of plantation land by Tan Ngun Ha, Tan Ah Loo and Heng Tooan to Captain James Pearl in May 1822. While there was no documentation of the dialect group of these planters, the transcription of their Chinese names suggested these names to be of Teochew origin. In Phua Chay Leong's book *The Teo-chews in Malaya*, Singapore was a fishing village with a Malay ruler residing near Keppel Harbour before Raffles' arrival. When a dozen or so Teochews from Haiyang first landed in Singapore, they were harassed by the natives and they called for support from fellow Teochews in Siam. Together with the arrivals from Siam, the Teohew community resided in "*sua kia teng*" (山仔顶) or present day Chulia Street area, close to the location of Wak Hai Cheng Bio.

Soon after the first sailing ship arrived from Amoy in Singapore in 1821, the Teochew red-bow junks also made their way here. Migration to Singapore grew rapidly and by 1827, the population of Singapore was estimated to be 13,732 with the Chinese being the majority ethnic group on the island. John Crawfurd, the second British Resident of Singapore, noted in 1827 that the "most numerous" within the Chinese community was "a race of fishermen from the sea-coast of the Province of Canton" which Walter Makepeace later speculated to be "Teo-chius" in the 1921 book *One Hundred Years Of Singapore*. In J. R. Logan's 1848 *Journal of the Indian Archipelago and Eastern Asia*, an article "The Chinese In Singapore" by Seah Eu Chin estimated the Chinese population to be around 40,000, of which 19,000 or almost half were Teochews, with the remaining made up of Hokkiens, Malacca-born, Cantonese, Hakkas and Hainanese.

The surge of Chinese immigrants to Singapore after the second half of the nineteenth century was due to a confluence of factors. Singapore became a crown colony in 1867 and the Singapore economy, established on the foundation of a trading port, expanded rapidly with the opening of the Suez Canal in 1869 which greatly reduced travel time between Europe and Asia. Sea travel was also made faster and more frequent with the conversion from wind-dependent sailing ships to steamships. Economic growth fuelled the demand for labour and the 1860 Treaty of Tientsin signed between the Qing government and western powers lifted the ban on Chinese immigration and opened up Shantou as a port for the export of Chinese labour to European colonies in Southeast Asia and other parts of the world. However, growth in the number of Hokkiens and Cantonese immigrants from mid-19th century outpaced the growth in Teochew immigrants and the Teochew majority was being eroded away. By the time the first systematic population census was undertaken in 1871, where the Chinese were accounted for by dialect groups, the Hokkiens had overtaken the Teochews as the largest dialect group in Singapore. In the 1911 census, taken almost 100 years after the founding of Singapore, the Teochews became the third largest dialect group after the Hokkiens and Cantonese and remained so till the 1957 census. From then until the 2010 census, the Hokkiens continue to be the largest Chinese dialect group at two-fifth of the Chinese population while the Teochews form the second largest group at approximately one-fifth of the Chinese population.

Teochew Enclaves in Singapore

It is said that wherever the waters meet land, the Teochews would be there. This is true in Singapore, where many Teochews were found residing, conducting businesses or eking out a living near rivers or the sea. Within the municipal limits of the Singapore town, the Teochews were known to live and conduct business activities south of the Singapore River in the Boat Quay and Ellenborough Market areas as well as north of the river in the North Boat Quay, River Valley Road, Hill Street and Beach Road vicinities. The two earliest areas occupied by the Teochews were the Philip Street/Kling Street (renamed Chulia Street in 1924) area and the Hill Street/River Valley Road area, nicknamed "*Suan Gian Dêng*" (山仔顶) and "*Uang Gê Suan Ka*" (皇家山脚) respectively.

PARTICULARS OF CHINESE POPULATION.

	1881			1891			1901			1911*		
	M.	F.	Total.	M.	F.	Total.	M.	F.	Total.	M.	F.	Total.
Cantonese	9,699	5,154	14,853	15,750	7,647	23,397	19,963	10,766	30,729	28,934	18,566	47,500
Hailam	8,266	53	8,319	8,596	115	8,711	9,237	214	9,451	10,206	298	10,504
Hing-Hoa	—	—	—	—	—	—	—	—	—	1,872	53	1,925
Hok-Chhia	—	—	—	—	—	—	—	—	—	3,564	76	3,640
Hok-Chiu	—	—	—	—	—	—	12,711	177	12,888	3,466	187	3,653
Hokkien	23,327	1,654	24,981	41,776	4,080	45,856	49,061	10,056	59,117	68,370	22,378	90,748
Kheh	5,561	609	6,170	6,558	844	7,402	7,252	1,262	8,514	9,516	2,431	11,947
Straits-born	4,513	5,014	9,527	6,084	6,721	12,805	7,719	7,779	15,498	20,369	23,193	43,562
Teo-chiu	20,946	1,698	22,644	21,682	2,055	23,737	24,186	3,378	27,564	29,705	7,708	37,413
Others	—	—	—	—	—	—	—	—	—	358	60	418
Not stated	259	13	272	—	—	—	238	42	280	—	—	—
Total	72,571	14,195	100,446	100,446	21,462	121,908	130,367	33,674	164,041	161,648	57,929	219,577

* The figures for 1911 (except for Straits-born, others, and total) are the numbers of persons speaking the particular Chinese dialect.

Breakdown of the Singapore Chinese population by dialect groups from 1881-1911. The first systematic population census in 1871 was taken as part of the Straits Settlement Census.

Plantation

When Raffles arrived in Singapore in 1819, there were already a number of gambier plantations on the island. A native of the Malay archipelago, gambier's economic value lay in its medicinal use in China and its use in the British dyeing and tanning industry and was an important cash crop in 19th century Singapore economy. Gambier was grown alongside pepper as they share a symbiotic relationship where gambier remains act as natural fertilisers for pepper plants.

GW Earl, who visited Singapore from 1832-34, observed that at the back of the town "on the bank of the creek are many plantations of pepper and gambier". Gambier plantations were initially located at Mount Stamford, River Valley Road, Bukit Timah Road and Selegie Hill but the growing demand for gambier as an export from Singapore to England in the mid- 1830s encouraged the Chinese to grow gambier more extensively especially in the under-developed interior. By 1836 it was estimated that there were at least 200 gambier plantations taking up a total of 2,350 acres of land and generated 22,000 piculs of produce annually. The average plantation produced 100 to 110 piculs of gambier and employed no more than six coolies at wages ranging from 4 to 41/2 Spanish dollar each. In 1841, the Chinese planters owned an estimated 500 plantations with an aggregate annual production of 60,000 piculs of gambier and 15,000 piculs of pepper. By 1848, gambier and pepper plantations took up three quarters of cultivated land and three-fifth of agricultural export in Singapore, with the Teochews making up the majority of the Chinese planters and coolies engaged in the industry. Chinese who made their fortune with gambier included Seah Eu Chin, Chan Ah Lak, Soh Tye Whoy, Yeo Ah Chong and Low Ah Choon. Seah Eu Chin's wealth from gambier established him not only as the leader of the Teochew community, but also a leader of the Chinese community and he was made a Justice of the Peace in 1867.

While gambier and pepper was an engine of economic growth for the young colony, the cultivation of gambier and pepper also played a key role in the expansion of the Singapore settlement beyond the southern tip of the island and it also led to the opening up of Johore. Gambier is a land-exhaustive crop and a typical plantation would survive only 20 years before the soil was depleted of nutrients. Increased demand and soil depletion in older gambier plantations resulted in the clearing of more jungle land to create more plantation land, paving the way for future development in northern Singapore.

Table 6: Population Engaged in Gambier and Pepper Cultivation

Year	Plantations	Workers
1836	250	2,250
1839	350	3,150
1840	477	4,293
1841	500	4,500
1848	800	7,200
1850	400	3,600
1855	543	4,887

Source: Phua Chay Leong (1993). *Selected Essays By Teochew Chinese In Singapore And Malaysia*. Singapore: Global Publishing.

Table 7: Production (including Johore) and Export of Gambier and Pepper in Singapore

	Gambier			Pepper		
Year	Imported	Produced	Exported	Imported	Produced	Exported
1850-51	25,267	110,654	135,921	19,287	44,219	63,506
1851-52	13,639	110,995	124,634	18,161	51,203	69,364
1852-53	12,025	113,822	125,817	19,276	45,681	54,956
1853-54	23,295	130,075	153,370	18,780	49,822	68,602

Source: The Straits Times, 15 May 1855.

Coolies in a gambier plantation. Gambier is prepared by boiling the leaves and twigs to extract their juice. The juice would be made into a concentrated form which was then pressed into moulds before being dried into blocks. As gambier leaves deteriorated within 24 hours of plucking, gambier processing facilities were located within the plantations in order to extract the best value from the leaves.

Lim Nee Soon posing with a full load of pineapple in a lorry marked Lim Nee Soon Rubber Factory (1916). Lim made his fortune in both rubber and pineapple plantations.

When arable land eventually ran out in Singapore, plantation activities moved further north into Johore especially with the introduction of the Johore kangchu system which encouraged the Teochew planters to open up uninhabited jungle hinterland. By January 1846, a number of Chinese planters from Singapore had moved into Johore and opened up gambier and pepper plantations financed by Singapore merchants, and the gambier produce was sent to Singapore for export. Singapore became the main centre for the gambier and pepper trade where gambier produce was imported from plantations in the Riau islands and Johore and then re-exported, in addition to the produce from the local plantations. In 1848 there were an estimated 200 gambier dealers with trading houses located at Boat Quay, North Boat Quay, Hill Street and the Ellenborough Market area. Tan Yeok Nee and Wee Ah Hood were Teochews who accumulated vast wealth from their ventures in Johore.

Starting from the late 19th century, the Singapore gambier and pepper industry began its decline with cultivated area dropping from 11,000 acres in 1890 to 6,000 acres in 1906 to 600 acres in 1912 and completely disappeared eventually. The two main factors responsible for this decline were the lack of arable land and the drop in demand for gambier products due to the presence of chemical replacements. Instead, these plantation crops were replaced by pineapple and rubber. The growing motor car industry created a huge global demand for rubber tyres and canned pineapple was a popular product in the European markets. While the Hokkiens were the main players in the rubber industry, some Teochew entrepreneurs were able to cash in on the new boom. Lim Nee Soon bought and converted large tracts of former gambier and pepper plantation into pineapple and rubber plantations and was so successful in his pineapple cultivation business that he became known as the "Pineapple King". Current day Yishun estate is where some of Lim Nee Soon's plantations used to stand. Leow Chia Heng was also known to have established his fortune in the rubber industry and up till the 1980s, a village bearing his namesake Kampong Chia Heng stood in the Yishun area.

EDUCATION

For centuries, the Teochews have drawn inspiration in education from the works of Han Yu, the Tang literati and Confucian scholar who promoted Han Chinese education when he was residing in Chaozhou. Han Yu was regarded as the pioneer in the propagation of Confucian orthodoxy in Chaozhou. Since then, Chaozhou had produced hundreds of scholars who made it to the *Jinshi* (进士) level, the highest title or "degree" to be attained in the imperial examination system. The emphasis and recognition given to education and scholastic achievement by the Chaozhou people can be seen by the number of gateway arches engraved with the names of imperial scholars which line the main street of Chaozhou City. It was recorded that at its peak the city had 103 of such arches.

In the 19th century, most of the Teochews who moved to Singapore were single male immigrants engaged in menial work with no means to raise families there. Those who did have their families in Singapore tended be better-off and could afford to engage private tutors or send their children to private schools. Females accounted for only 12% of the Teochew population in 1901 but rose to 20% in 1911, and the numbers continued to grow over the next few decades, implying the growing presence of families and children. Around the same time, overseas Chinese began to be influenced by the Reformist Movement of 1898 and the idea of establishing public schools to educate the masses took root. Tuan Mong School was the first public school set up by the Teochew community in 1906 and, since then, the Teochews have set up large and small education institutions for both boys and girls, covering all levels from primary to tertiary education. The Teochews were also pioneers in the provision of bilingual education to girls from Chinese families in Singapore.

In 1628, during the Ming dynasty, eight men from Chaozhou became Jinshis at the same examination and they came to be known later as the Eight Luminaries of Wuchen (戊辰八贤), wuchen being the year 1628 in the Chinese calendar.

Students of Tuan Mong School with their teachers (1910) at the school's first location 52 Hill Street. The Qing dynasty national flag, the Dragon Flag, is in the background.

Tuan Mong School and Ngee Ann Secondary

Concerned about the lack of education opportunities for a growing number of Teochew children in Singapore, a group of 26 Teochews including Tan Hoon Chew, Liau Chia Heng, Chua Chu Yong and Yeo Chan Boon donated $30,000 in 1906 to set up a school for the community. Named the Singapore Teochew Tuan Mong School (新加坡潮州公立端蒙学堂), it started off in a rented shophouse at Hill Street. Within a year enrolment doubled from an initial 68 students to 146 students, and the school moved to its own premises near Read Bridge in the Clarke Quay area in 1913. By 1916 the student population reached 265 and bigger school premises was required. In 1917 the existing premises was sold for $65,000 and 97 Tank Road was purchased for $52,500. The school moved into Tank Road in June 1918. A branch was set up at 33 Minto Road (in the Kampong Java area) in 1919 at the advocacy of Teo Eng Hock, and by 1928 the student population reached 748 at the main school and 300 at the Minto Road branch. Classes were initially conducted in the Teochew dialect. Mandarin was introduced in 1918 as "national language" lessons, but by 1937, all classes were taught in Mandarin except for the English language subject.

In 1953, Ngee Ann Kongsi took over the management of the school and the school properties. Tuan Mong High School (端蒙中学) was established in 1955 to support the growing demand for higher education and by the late 1950s, the school grew to be one of the three largest Chinese schools in Singapore together with the Chinese High School and Chung Cheng High School. The school had more than 2,000 students in 1961 and plans were made to rebuild the Tank Road

Ngee Ann Girls' School at 299 River Valley Road. Teo Yeonh Huai Kuan is the current owner and occupier of the building.

Ann Primary School building was ready by November 2000. Although Ngee Ann Primary School is a government-aided school, Ngee Ann Kongsi continues to subsidise some of the school's facilities and its members sit on the school's management committee.

Other Schools

Other Teochew organizations also involved in establishing schools in Singapore included Teochew *shantang* (善堂) and clan associations. Seng Siang Society of the Thong Kheng Charitable Institution (同敬善堂诚善社) set up Thong Keng School at Kallang Road which later moved to the Geylang area before the school closed in 1981. From 1946 to 1975, Nam Ann Siang Theon (南安善堂) operated Nam Ann School at Ah Hood Road to serve the children living in the Balestier area. The predecessor of Kityang Kwee Lim Low Clan Association set up Guilin School (桂林学校) in Geyland Serai before WWII and after the War the school because Hwa Nong School (华农学校). Chao Yang School (朝阳学校) was formed in 1953 by Teo Yeonh Huai Kuan in the clan association's premises at 341 Clemenceau Avenue. An extended school block and sports facilities were added in 1958 to handle the increased number of students. The school population began to decline during the 1970s and was forced to close in 1982. The Clemenceau Avenue premises was used by the Singapore Association for Educationally Sub-Normal Children to set up Chaoyang Special School, and it was demolished in the 1980s due to the construction of the Central Tunnel Expressway (CTE).

The Teochew organisations were not the only ones to set up facilities to address the lack of educational opportunities for the community in colonial Singapore. Individuals and small groups were also involved in forming or running small "private" schools to provide elementary education in underserved areas, especially where there was a sizeable Teochew population. These schools were mostly privately funded by socially-conscious individuals with a strong desire to provide education to children and were mostly small operations often administrated without the support of a board of directors. In some cases the school founder would also double up as the school's principal and even teacher. For example, in the Teochew enclave of the Ellenborough Market area *Lin Jingsong* (林景崧) founded *Shuren* School (树人学校) in 1923 as a one-classroom school in a rented shophouse at Keng Cheow Street. Another such school in the area was Tuan Eng School (陶英学校) set up in 1940 by *Lin Chunli* (林春李) at Read Street.

Chao Yang School and Teo Yeonh Huai Kuan on Clemenceau Avenue.

Sin Hua School in the 1970s. The school relocated to new premises at Hougang Ave 1 in 1985.

Kheng Cheng School graduating class of 1961 at the Derbyshire Road premises.

A number of schools affiliated with the Teochews were also found in the Sembawang area where there were large rural settlements of Teochews. The first school in the region was *Fachu* School (发初学校) set up in 1919 by Lim Nee Soon who donated both land and money for the school. Fachu was also the alternate name of Lim Nee Soon. The school name was changed to *Zhanhua* School (湛华学校) in the 1930s and, in 1940, *Zhanhua* School combined with *Qizhi* School (启智学校) to form Poi Eng Public School. At Bah Soon Pah, the Teochew residents set up *Huashun* School (华顺学校) to educate Teochew children in the village while the Hokkiens set up *Jiannan* School (建南学校) for the Hokkien students. The dialect divide was broken in 1946 when both schools combined to form Hwa Nam School (华南学校). Kwang Teck School (广德学校) in Chye Kay Village was set up by Lim Sioh in 1939 on land donated by Ngee Ann Kongsi.

Other Teochew affiliated schools set up before the Japanese Occupation were Seak Tiat School (植哲学校), *Shentaihai* School (沈泰海学校), Nanyang Commercial School (南洋商科学校), Lee Sin School (励新学校), Nam King School (南强学校) and Hoo Neu School (辅女学校). These pre-war schools were very active in supporting the Singapore Chinese community's anti-Japanese aggression cause in China and the students were often involved in events to raise money for the cause. Many of these early Chinese schools closed down in the second half of the 20th century.

Sing Hua School (公立醒华学校) and Kheng Cheng School (擎青学校) are remaining representatives of the various grassroots schools set up by the Chinese community to provide educational opportunities to children in rural areas.

In 1930, Chua Cheok Sar set up Sing Hua Public School in a wood-and-thatch building at Lim Tua Tow Road which was rented from the Sze Hai Tong Bank. The school was officially registered in 1932. During the Japanese Occupation, the school halted operations but resumed classes after the war. When Chua passed away in 1949, his son Chua Tiah Seng continued his father's mission of providing education to the rural children population and served as the school's principal from 1949 to 1976. Sing Hua became an aided school in 1957, and then an integrated institution with both Chinese and English as the medium of instruction in 1973. A new school building at Lim Tua Tow was opened in 1975. In 1985, the school moved to Hougang Ave 1 and its name was changed to Xinghua Primary School. Charlton School and Parry Primary School were merged with the school in 2003 and 2007 respectively.

In 1927 Mdm Lim Peng Tuan, a horticulture nursery operator, set up Kheng Cheng School at 219 Moulmein Road with Tan Cheo Teng as the school's first principal. The name "Kheng Cheng" means to "uplift the youths" in Teochew as Mdm Lim believed in educating and mentoring young people. For years prior to Kheng Cheng School's formal registration, Tan and Mdm Lim had been running an informal school to educate children in the area around lower Thomson Road. The school moved to 6/6A Derbyshire Road in 1937 to accommodate more students but the school building was destroyed during World War II. It was rebuilt after the War, but in the 1960s, with new families moving into new towns the school made a decision to relocate.

The school Management Committee managed to raise funds for a new building and in August 1972, the new school building in Toa Payoh was officially opened. When the 30-year lease was up in Toa Payoh, MOE agreed to the construction of a new building on the same site. The current school building at Lorong 3 Toa Payoh was officially opened on 19 November 2005 by the then Minister for Education, Mr Tharman Shanmugaratnam.

take care of their entertainment needs. Teochew-affiliated recreation clubs included Chui Huay Lim Club formed in the mid 1800s, Sek Kho Club (适可俱乐部) formed in 1929 and Teo Chew Lian Kheow Club (潮州联侨俱乐部) formed in 1938. The most established cultural institution formed by the Teochews are the amateur opera associations. Supported mostly by Teochew businessmen or middle class Teochews, these organisations were formed to play and sing Waijiang Opera (外江戏) or Han Opera (汉剧) to differentiate themselves from the mass-appeal Teochew opera performed by professional troupes. The leading associations formed were Er Woo Amateur Musical and Dramatic Association (余娱儒乐社) in 1912, Lak Aik Amateur Musical & Dramatic Association (六一儒乐社) in 1929, Thau Yong Amateur Musical Association (陶融儒乐社) in Aug 1931, Chenh Hua Amateur Musical Association (星华儒剧社) in 1935 and Nam Hua Amateur Musical and Dramatic Association (南华儒剧社) in 1963. Er Woo's past presidents included Lim Nee Soon and Tan Cheng Hean. These associations often staged single or joint performances to raise funds for various causes.

Song Dafeng (宋大峰), the patron deity for the Teochew shantangs. Born Lin Ling-e (林灵噩) into a wealthy family in Fujian province in 1039, he was appointed a magistrate but grew disillusioned with corruption and resigned from his official post to become a nomadic monk. When he arrived in 1120 at the town of Heping (和平), Chaoyang county, the place was suffering from drought and a plague epidemic. He offered prayers for the well-being of the townsfolk and concocted medicine to be distributed freely to the sick. He also embarked on a project to build a bridge across a busy river nearby to make river crossing safer, but unfortunately, he died of exhaustion in 1153 before the bridge could be completed. Touched by his compassion, the public built a temple, Baode Hall (报德堂), in his honour.

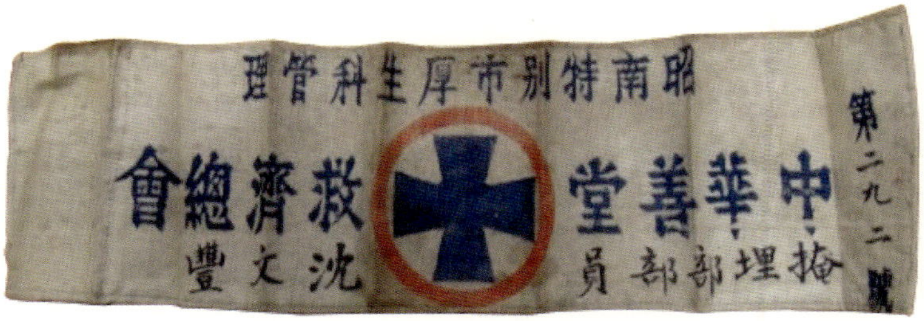

Label issued to a member of the burial unit from the Blue Cross Charitable Organisation during the Japanese Occupation.

Shantang

Shantangs (善堂, Charity Hall) are traditional charity organisations blending philanthropy, religion and after-life affairs into one culture and are closely associated with the Teochews in Singapore. The culture marries Confucianism's filial piety values and Buddhism's teaching of universal welfare with Chinese folk religion's practice of deity worship. Welfare societies looking after the old and sickly had existed in Chaozhou since the Ming dynasty and it was not uncommon for local merchants to establish charity halls to build roads and bridges, in addition to providing medical care, food and coffins for the needy. It is estimated that at least 161 charity halls existed in the Chaozhou region from 1876 to the Republic period.

The first Teochew shantang in Singapore was Seu Teck Sean Tong Yiang Sin Sia (修德善堂养心社) formed in 1915 by *Chen Sishun* (陈四顺), *Wu Lisheng* (吴立声), *Yang Yongchao* (杨永潮) and *Chen Rong'an* (陈荣安) in a shophouse at River Valley Road with "joss ash" brought over from Dawu Xiude Shantang (大吴修德善堂) in Fuyangzhen (浮洋镇), Chao'an. This was followed by Phoh Kiu Siang-tng (普救善堂) in 1929, Nanyang Thong Hong Siang-tng (南洋同奉善堂) in 1930, Seng Siang Society of the Thong Kheng Charitable Institution (同敬善堂诚善社) in 1943 and Nam Ann Siang Theon (南安善堂) in 1944.

Early Teochew immigrants to Singapore were not only concerned about their livelihood but also about the issues of aging, sickness and death, especially when they did not have family members with them here or could not make the journey back to China. The shantangs' early role was to address these concerns through the provision of medical services, coffin donation and funeral assistance. These services proved to be indispensable during the Japanese Occupation which also became a turning point for the shantangs' operations. The Syonan government halted almost all activities by social organisations except for those related to welfare activities. The Teochew shantangs were permitted to operate to provide medical care and food and were known for taking care of the dead by collecting corpses and providing the necessary coffins and burials. These services extended beyond dialect, racial and religious lines and, for the first time, the shantangs reached out to the general public in Singapore beyond the Teochew community. Five of them joined together to form the Chinese Charitable Institutions Union (中华善堂救济总会) and the Japanese government even exempted shantang volunteers from other services to the government and membership for these five shantangs surged to 3,000 during this period.

Membership badge of the scripture and music department in Bukit Timah Seu Teck Sean Tong.

After World War II, the Chinese Charitable Institutions Union was renamed the Blue Cross Charitable Institution (中华善堂蓝十救济总会) and continued to be the umbrella organisation for the charitable works of the shantangs, and the "blue cross" became the emblem of the shantangs' philanthropic efforts. Between 1960 and 1980, five more shantangs, Thong Teck Sian Tong Lian Sin Sia (同德善堂念心社), Poh Teck Siang-tng (报德善堂), Nam Hong Siang Theon (南凤善堂), Cheng Hong Siang-tng (众弘善堂) and Chung Hong Siang-tng (崇峰善堂), joined the Institution.

The shantangs in Singapore are unlike ordinary Chinese temples as they are formally organised with a focus on performing charity in addition to providing religious services. The typical shantang consists of three main departments: a welfare department to manage the charity work and affiliated charity organisations; the altar hall department (堂事股) to take charge of religious work including taking care of the altars and providing religious books (mainly Buddhist) for free distribution; and the department of scripture and music (经乐股) to take charge of teaching Buddhist chants, scriptures, and traditional music used during funerals and religious occasions.

A welfare service provided by a shantang is the provision of free Traditional Chinese Medicine (TCM) consultation and medicine and many shantangs continue to provide this service. In recent years, Toa Payoh Seu Teck Sean Tong and Thong Teck Sian Tong Lian Sin Sia have also collaborated with the National Kidney Foundation to set up dialysis centres. On Chinese New Year and on occasions of major shantang celebrations, red packets are distributed to the aged and the needy. Some shantangs also set up welfare facilities to take care of the needy in Singapore and even established separate welfare organisations registered with the National Council of Social Services to provide stronger governance of donations and their charity work. Examples of such organisations are Thong Kheng Welfare Service Society, Nam Hong Welfare Service Society and Cheng Hong Welfare Service Society

One important aspect of the shantangs' service to the community is the provision of traditional funeral rites and post-funeral support to the families of deceased members. Teochews, like most Chinese, place heavy emphasis on the Confucian value of filial piety and ancestral reverence, and the shantangs provide both the services and facilities to support this value. Shantangs are known for conducting traditional funeral services known as "merit service" or "*gong dêg*" (功德) for the deceased. Of Buddhist origin, the "*gong dêg*" session is performed as a means of salvation for the deceased's soul and consists of a series of rituals alongside the chanting of Buddhist scriptures and Confucian teachings to the accompaniment of traditional Teochew music. The scriptures and rituals extol the family members to be grateful to their parents and emphasise the virtues of filial piety and remembering one's roots. A number of shantangs also operate columbaria and ancestral halls to house cremated remains and ancestral tablets of the deceased, in addition to conducting regular prayer sessions for the deceased. The

ACTIVITIES

As with the many immigrant communities to Singapore, the Teochews have contributed to building schools and erecting social institutions to serve the education and social support needs of their community and the larger Singapore society. However it is in the areas of politics, the visual arts and philanthropy where their presence and impact outweigh their representation in the Singapore population.

Politics

Singapore's founding Prime Minister Lee Kuan Yew commented in the 1998 book *Lee Kuan Yew: The Man and His Ideas* on the disproportionate number of Teochews in the Singapore cabinet. "Look at the number of smart Teochews there are … just count them. Teo Chee Hean, Lim Hng Kiang, George Yeo, Lim Boon Heng. Is it a coincidence? In a Cabinet of 15, how do you explain that?" At the time of the book's publication, the Singapore cabinet had 12 Chinese ministers of whom five were Teochews which include Lee Boon Yang in addition to the four names mentioned by Lee Kuan Yew. This was not the first time in Singapore's political history where Teochew representation outnumbered its 20% representation in the Chinese population. In the 1955 landmark Legislative Assembly election where Lee Kuan Yew won his first election in the ward of Tanjong Pagar, a total of 16 Chinese were elected into the Legislative Assembly with him, and half of these elected Chinese were Teochews representing various political parties.

The Teochews had actively participated in Singapore's administration since its early colonial days. The British government established the Straits Settlements as a separate Crown Colony on 1 April 1867 ruled by a governor with the assistance of an executive council and a Legislative Council. The colonial government engaged the Chinese community by appointing selected Chinese to positions in the Legislative Council and later the Chinese Advisory Board. Seah Liang Seah was the second Chinese to be appointed as a member of the legislative council in 1883 and he also served as a Municipal Commissioner and a member of the Chinese Advisory Board. In 1872 Tan Seng Poh became the first Chinese to be a Municipal Commissioner. The Teochews' influence in 19th century Singapore was summed by a Teochew phrase "The Tans blanketed the sky (world), Chua ruled the grounds and Seah is the emperor." (陈天蔡地佘皇帝). According to renown historian Prof Hsu Yun Tsiao, the phrase refers to prominent Teochew merchants such as Tan Seng Poh and Tan Yeok Nee who dominated the gambier and opium trade, Chua Moh Choon who was the leader of secret society Ghee Hok Kongsee and Seah

Eu Chin who was appointed as a senior member of the jury council and presided over many local lawsuits in 19th century Singapore.

In 1889, then Governor of the Straits Settlement Sir Cecil Clementi set up the Chinese Advisory Board in Singapore to facilitate communication between the colonial government and the Chinese community. The board consisted of the Chinese Protector and a body of representative Chinese from various dialect groups to advise the colonial government on Chinese affairs. The Teochews were assigned five out of seventeen places on the Chinese board, and early Teochew representatives were Seah Liang Seah, Tan Yong Siak, Low Cheang Yee and Koo Ngee Choo. Other Teochews who served on the board later included Lau Long Teng (1921), Leow Chia Heng (1921-1929), Seah Eng Tong (1921–1941), Tan Thuan Hian (1921–1925), Heng Pang Kiat (1922–1929), Tan Tsz Yew (1924–1930), Tan Guan Chua (1929–1941), Lee Wee Nam (1930–1941), Lee Kim Soo (1931–1934), Low Peng Soy (1934–1938), Tan Chin Hian (1937–1939) and Lim Soo Siam (1938–1941).

As Singapore moved towards self-government and independence, the Teochews became heavily involved in Singapore's post-war political scene. The first general election in Singapore was held on 20 March 1948, when six of the 22 seats on the Legislative Council became directly-elected as provided under the 1947 Singapore Legislative Council Elections Ordinance. While voting eligibility was limited to registered adult voters over the age of 21 who had been British subjects for at least a year prior to the election, it was nevertheless a milestone in the political history of Singapore. The Progressive Party led by Tan Chye Cheng won three out of the six seats. Tan, son of Tan Guan Chua, founded the Progressive Party with John Laycock and Nazir Ahmad Mallal in August 1947 and became the party's first president. Tan was elected for the Municipal South-West division in 1948 and the Tanglin division in the 1951 election.

Tan Chye Cheng (c. 1970s). Tan was the only Chinese elected into the Legislative Council during Singapore's first general election in 1948.

The Rendel Commission Report of 1954 paved the way for internal self-government in Singapore by recommending constitutional reforms that increased local participation in politics. Two key recommendations of the report was the automatic registration of voters and the transformation of the Legislative Council into a Legislative Assembly with majority of its members elected. With most of the recommendations accepted, the Rendel Constitution was implemented by the Colony Order-in-Council of 1955. On 2 April 1955, the Legislative Assembly general election was held to elect 25 out of the 32 members and eight Teochews representing various political parties were elected. They were Goh Tong Liang, Lim Koon Teck and Lim Choon Mong for the Progressive Party; Lim Cher Kheng for the Democratic Party; Seah Peng Chuan, Tan Theng Chiang and Lee Choon Eng for the Labour Front; and Goh Chew Chua for the People's Action Party.

Since Singapore's independence, many Teochews have been elected into the Singapore parliament and continue to contribute to Singapore's nation building. Then Deputy Prime Minister Lee Hsien Loong commented in his speech at the opening of the 12th Teochew International Convention in 2003 that "out of 19 full Cabinet Ministers, seven, or about one-third, are Teochews. In Parliament, out of a House of 94 members, close to 30, also about one-third, are Teochews. This is well above their proportion in the population, which is about 15%." Past cabinet ministers of Teochew ethnicity included Yeo Cheow Tong, Yeo Ning Hong, Lee Boon Yang, George Yeo, Lim Hwee Hua and Lim Boon Heng. Lim Hwee Hua became Singapore's first female Cabinet minister when she was appointed Minister in the Prime Minister's Office in 2009. As of September 2017, full ministers who are Teochews are Teo Chee Hean (Deputy Prime Minister and Coordinating Minister for National Security), Lim Hng Kiang (Minister for Trade and Industry (Trade)), Lim Swee Say (Minister for Manpower), Ng Chee Meng (Minister for

The "Tradition Unfettered" gallery at the Singapore National Gallery featuring local works using the Chinese ink-brush technique. About two-fifths of the artists featured in the gallery are Teochews, including Chen Wen Hsi, Chen Chong Swee, Tan Kian Por, Henry Chen Kezhan, Fan Chang Tien, Lee Hock Moh, Nai Swee Leng, Tan Oe Pang, Chua Ek Kay and Tang Dawu.

drawing were electives. The academy registered more than 50 students but it unfortunately closed within 2 years. Nevertheless its founding was a milestone in the establishment of a modern structured curriculum in Singapore's art education.

Teochew artists also took it upon themselves to nurture art talent in Singapore. The family of Chen Chong Swee provided support for art education by donating his art works to raise funds. In 1994, Sotheby's held the Chen Chong Swee Charity Auction and sold 138 of the 151 paintings donated by Chen's family members. The auction raised more than $700,000 for the Chen Chong Swee Art Scholarship fund that is managed by the National Arts Council (NAC). In 2012 Chen's family made a gift to establish The Chen Chong Swee Asian Art Programme at Yale–NUS College to promote the appreciation of local and regional art among students. The programme also supports a postgraduate scholarship for students to study fine art at select institutions. As an arts advocate, Chen had called for the creation of a national art gallery and collection. In 1998, while in the midst of the Asian financial crisis, Henri Chen organised an exhibition in which part of the proceeds from the sale of the exhibited works went towards establishing the Visual Arts Fund (VAF). In 2009, Henri Chen established a private non-profit organisation now known as the Temenggong Artists-In-Residence (Temenggong) to manage an arts residency programme for foreign artists and to promote cross-cultural exchanges and networking between foreign and local artists. In the late 1980s, Tang Da Wu founded the first art colony in Singapore, The Artists Village, to encourage artists to challenge the conventions and protocols of mainstream art practice, and members of the Village were among the first contemporary artists in Singapore to practise installation art and performance art.

Like many artists in Singapore, many Teochew artists taught in art schools and mentored generations of young artists. Jieyang-born pioneer artist Fan Chang Tien was an accomplished artist in China and Bangkok before coming to Singapore in 1956. His art and teaching inspired new directions and development for local Chinese ink painting. Among his protégés were Lim Cher Eng, Nai Swee Leng, Lim Kay Hiong, Tan Oe Pang, Tan Siow Aik, Low Eng, Ng Yong Choon, Lee Soo Chee, Henri Chen and Chua Ek Kay. Chen Chong Swee taught in Tao Nan School, Tuan Mong High School, Chinese High School

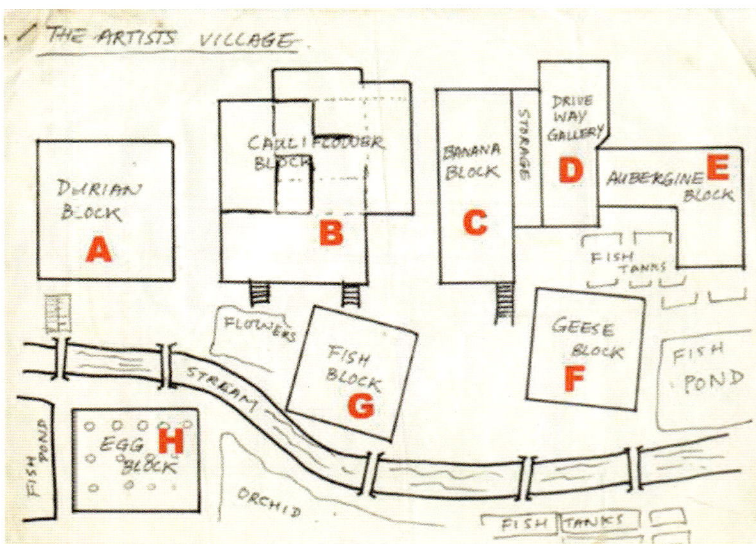

Tang Da Wu found the studio space at 61B Lorong Gambas in 1988, later named as The Artists Village in Jan 1989. The Artists Village moved out in Mar 1990. The Artists Village was officially registered as a society in Feb 1992.

and Chung Cheng High School, and in 1951, he became the head of the Chinese painting department at NAFA where he taught for the next 24 years. In 1982, the Ministry of Education started a four-year Art in Education Diploma Course for secondary school art teachers to raise the standard of art education in public schools. Choo Keng Kwang not only oversaw the programme but was its main lecturer and he trained up to 80% of the art teachers in Singapore.

Ngee Ann Cultural Centre, set up in 1998 by Ngee Ann Kongsi, engages the Teochew community and artists by promoting local and international cultural events such as Ngee Ann Photographic Exhibition, National Day Calligraphy and Painting Exhibition, Teochew Cultural Festival and National Teochew Calligraphy and Painting Exhibition, as well as organising activities related to Chinese calligraphy, paintings, Teochew opera and music. It also supports the larger arts community by offering exhibition space, facilities and organisational resources for local and international artistic and cultural activities. In addition Ngee Ann Kongsi provides scholarships and awards to students in LASALLE College of the Arts, Nanyang Academy of Fine Arts (NAFA) and School of the Arts, Singapore (SOTA). Since 2003, Teochew Poit Ip Huay Kuan has been organising regular Calligraphy and Painting Exchange gatherings where well-known calligraphers or ink painters are invited to give talks on specific topics. Each gathering would also host on-the-spot writing or painting sessions by speakers and participants so that all those who are present can learn from one another.

Art also serves as a means for Teochew artists to contribute to non-art charitable causes. Philanthropy within the Teochew cultural community is a tradition dating back to the early 20th century where amateur opera associations put up charity performances to raise funds for various relief efforts within the Chinese community. Choo Keng Kwang has donated his works to raise funds for charitable causes and organisations. For example, sales proceeds from his paintings were contributed to St. Andrew's Mission Hospital and Touch Community Services. He participated in the "Presidents' Charity Art Exhibition — Choo Keng Kwang: An Artistic Path of His Own", which managed to raise $160,000 for charity. In 1997, he donated oil paintings to the President's Star Charity Show. The sale of Choo's paintings for charitable causes has benefited community centres, institutions, associations, scholarships for the performing arts and even the ASEAN Secretariat office in Jakarta, Indonesia. Nai Swee Long donated up to 100 pieces to the Singapore Buddhist Federation Foundation in 1999 to support the fund-raising efforts of the foundation.

The Teochews' appreciation and love for art is reflected in the number of avid Chinese art collectors within the community, the most prominent being Dr Tan Tzse Chor, Low Chuck Tiew and Yeo Khee Lim. Dr Tan was a successful self-made entrepreneur and an accomplished calligrapher whose works were exhibited locally and abroad. He was a fervent art lover who made friends with Chinese artists such as Xu Beihong and Zhang Daqian, and he built up a collection of Chinese art works known as the Xiang Xue Zhuang Collection (香雪庄). He died in 1983, and in 2003 his family donated a portion of his prized collection to the Asian Civilization Museum where the museum was invited to handpick the collection's best works that included works by Xu Beihong, Ren Bonian, Qi Baishi and Wu Changshuo. Dr Tan had set up the Tan Tzse Chor Trust Fund with the Singapore Art Society in 1977 and it remains the longest surviving art award in Singapore. Low Chuck Tiew was sent by Sze Hai Tong Bank to work in Hong Kong and despite his limited financial resources, compiled a collection of works from the major schools of the Ming and Qing periods including the Wu School, the Songjiang School, the Four Monks, the Orthodox School and the Eight Eccentrics of Yangzhou

An accomplished artist in the Shanghai Xieyi (写意) style, Fan Chang Tien was responsible for grooming a generation of eminent ink and brush painters in Singapore. Among his protégés were Henri Chen, Chua Ek Kay, Lee Soo Chee, Ling Cher Eng, Lim Kay Hiong, Low Eng, Nai Swee Leng, Ng Yong Choon, Tan Oe Pang and Tan Siow Aik.

which he donated to the Hong Kong Museum of Art in 1989. At the time of its donation, the collection, valued at $150 million then, was billed as the most comprehensive collection of Chinese works outside mainland China and Taiwan. Known as the Xu Bai Zhai Collection (虚白斋) it is one of the Hong Kong Museum of Art's major collections and comprises of more than 600 representative works of Chinese painting and calligraphy . Yeo Khim Lim was a successful businessman who started art collecting by accident. Through a process of consultation and collaborative art appreciation sessions with Teochew artists and collectors, he amassed a large collection of Chinese ink brush paintings over a 40 years period. Coined the Xiu Hai Lou Collection (袖海楼) by Chen Chong Swee, it is the largest and most established private collection of Chinese painting and calligraphy in Singapore. Both Tan Tzse Chor and Yeo Khee Lim also gifted art works to the NUS Art Museum.

On an ongoing basis, Ngee Ann Kongsi is known to collect works of Teochew artists from both Singapore and the Chaoshan region regularly and the collection is exhibited in a gallery located within the Teochew Building. In August 2016, Ngee Ann Development, in which Ngee Ann Kongsi is a major shareholder, donated $16 million to the National Gallery Singapore to boost its research and curatorial work.

The Teochews' contribution and impact to the Singapore visual arts scene is multi-faceted and far-reaching. As artists, they form a bastion in preserving traditional Chinese art forms with a strong forte in works engaging the foundation of the ink-brush technique, but at the same they also challenge the conventions and protocols of mainstream art practices as the forerunners of styles such as the Nanyang school, social realism school and in contemporary installation art and performance art. As advocates, they have nurtured generations of Singapore artists through their roles as mentors and teachers and have set up scholarships and programmes at both institutional and individual levels to elevate the standard of art talent in Singapore. As art patrons, they were among the most well-known Singapore art collectors who supported both local and foreign artists and yet selflessly donated their prized collections to museums to be shared with the rest of the world.

Philanthropy

The Teochews have a long tradition of philanthropy dating back to the Ming dynasty where welfare societies in Chaozhou took care of society's old and sickly, and the practice continued into the Qing dynasty. It was not uncommon for merchants in Chaozhou to establish shantangs (善堂) to provide public services such as building roads and bridges, as well as providing medical care, food and coffins for the needy. The first shantang formed in Singapore was Seu Teck Sean Tong Yiang Sin Sia (修德善堂养心社) in 1915. Unlike modern philanthropic organisations which are funded by the wealth of private individuals or families, shantangs are community-based charity organisations where donors of varying wealth status contribute money and items towards a common purpose of helping the less fortunate in society. The shantangs were also among the earliest volunteer welfare organizations to recruit and mobilise volunteers on a large scale to perform public services, starting from their involvement in taking care of the dead during the Japanese Occupation in Singapore. Over their hundred year old presence in Singapore they have evolved from small outfits meeting the welfare needs of the Teochew community to structured welfare organizations registered with the National Council of Social Service to serve the under-privileged regardless of race or religion. Today the shantangs continue to provide charitable services under the emblem of the Blue Cross Charitable Organisation especially in the area of traditional Chinese medicine (TCM) services and in caring for the aged and handicapped.

Providing free funeral service is a Teochew shantang tradition dating back to the Ming period. Organizations such as Nam Hong Welfare Service Society and Cheng Hong Welfare Society let needy seniors sign up for the service and state their funeral preference while they are alive.

CULTURE

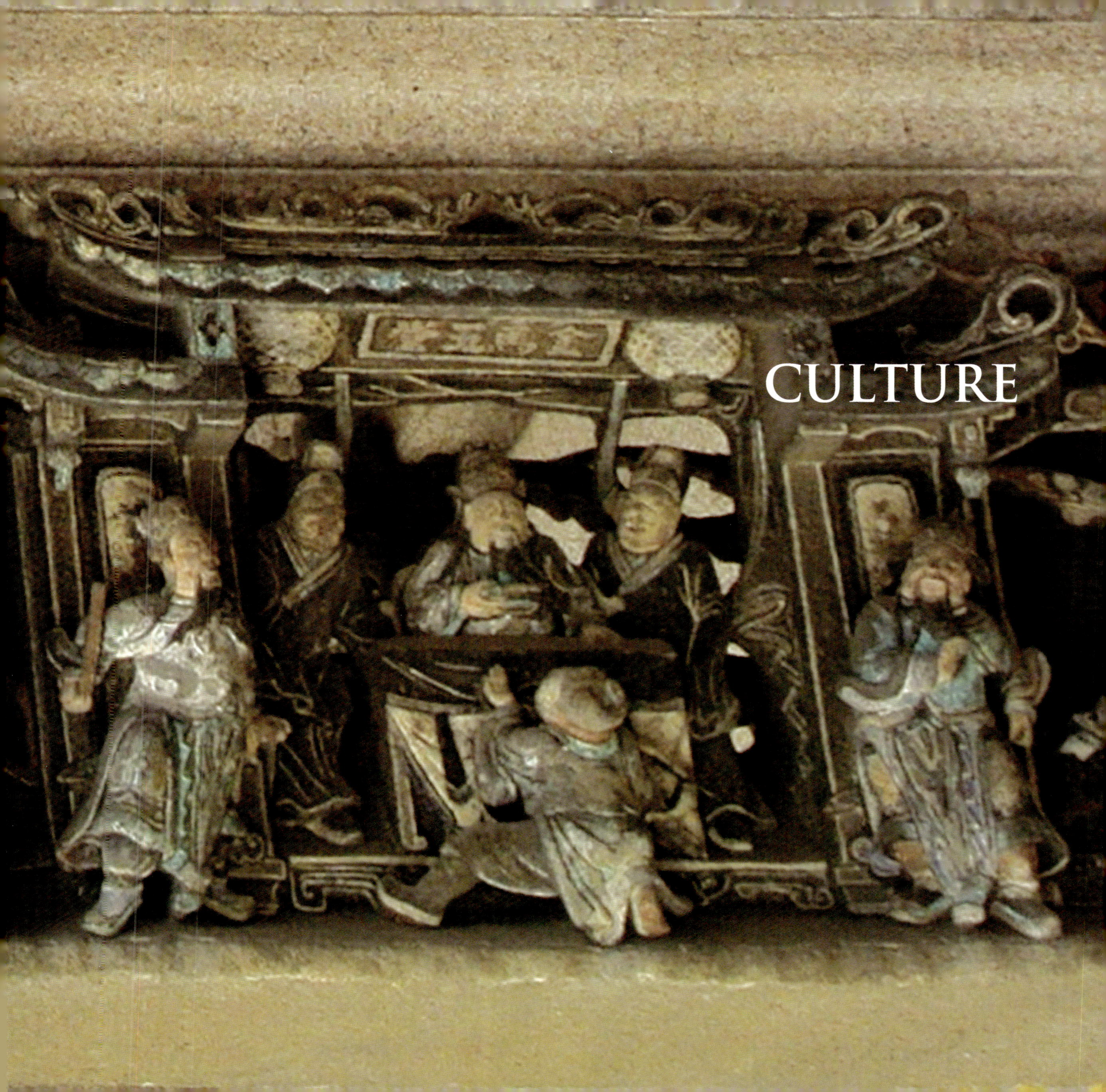

Beliefs, Customs and Practices

Teochew festive practices and celebrations are based on religious events and beliefs, passages of life and the important "Four Seasons and Eight Festivals" (四时八节) which traditionally for the Teochews refers to the eight seasonal festivals of Spring Festival or Chinese New Year, Yuanxiao Festival, Tomb Sweeping Day, Dragon Boat Festival, Hungry Ghost Festival, Mid-Autumn Festival, Double Nine Festival and Winter Solstice.

Ancestral Reverence

Teochews traditionally place a heavy emphasis on ancestral reverence, commonly termed as ancestral worship, which is the practice of living family members and descendants paying honour and respect to their ancestors. Deeply rooted in the Confucian value of filial piety, paying respect to one's ancestors is an expression of this value as it is believed that the relationship and obligations of latter generations toward earlier generations continue even after death. Ancestral reverence reminds living descendants of their roots and ancestry and on a larger scale, the practice serves to maintain kinship ties with fellow clansmen who share the same ancestry. The most important days associated with ancestral reverence are the "*Cêng Mêng*" festival (清明节, "Tomb Sweeping Day") and the "*Dang Zoih*" (冬节, Winter Solstice), though Teochews would also pay respects to their ancestors during most of the seasonal festivals.

In the Chaoshan region, ancestral halls are built to house the ancestral tablets of the clan's deceased members and remembrance sessions involving the entire clan are held regularly on these premises. The importance of the value of ancestral reverence was not lost to the Teochews even when they moved overseas. Ngee Ann Kongsi was established in the mid-19th century with the objective to promote and observe the rites, customs and religious beliefs of the Teochews

Clansmen gathering to pay respect to ancestors in the ancestral hall of the Xing (幸) clan in Oding, Chenghai (澄海鸥汀村).

Teochew Memorial Park in Yishun was set up by Ngee Ann Kongsi in remembrance of Teochews previously buried in the Kongsi's past cemeteries. The Kongsi continues the tradition of conducting an annual ceremony with other Teochew organizations to pay respect to the dead at the memorial park.

in Singapore, especially those related to funeral and burial affairs. The first cemetery set up by the Kongsi was Tai Shan Ting (泰山亭), a plot of land bordering Orchard Road, Paterson Road and Grange Road purchased from the East India Company in 1845. This was followed by more land acquisitions with the increasing number of Teochews in Singapore.

While there were other Teochew-owned public and private cemeteries, Ngee Ann Kongsi eventually became the largest owner of public burial sites for the Teochew community and by 1933 the Kongsi owned close to 363 acres of burial land all over Singapore. In addition to Tai Shan Ting, the Kongsi owned Guang Ren Shan (广仁山) at Mata Ikan Changi, Guang En Shan (广恩山) at Thomson Road near Tan Tock Seng Hospital, Guang Yi Shan (广义山) at Upper Serangoon Road, Guang Shou Shan (广寿山) at Bukit Timah Road (present site of Ngee Ann Polytechnic), Guang De Shan (广德山) at Sembawang and Guang Xiao Shan (广孝山) at Bukit Panjang.

As these early cemeteries started giving way to urban redevelopment starting from the mid-20th century, Ngee Ann Kongsi set up the Teochew Memorial Park in Yishun to house remains exhumed from these sites. In addition, the Kongsi operates the Teochew Funeral Parlour at Ubi Avenue 4 to continue its founding mission of preserving the funeral practices of the Teochew community after the original funeral parlour was acquired by the government together with the Kongsi's cemetery located at Upper Serangoon Road. Built in 1989, the Teochew Funeral Parlour is open to the public and not limited to Teochews.

Complementing the work of Ngee Ann Kongsi are the various shantangs or charity halls that provide the related Teochew funeral rites services. Teochews refer to these funeral rites as "*gong dêg*" (功德, "performing goodwill") which consists primarily of rituals and chants performed by priests with the participation of the deceased's family. The verses chanted during a "*gong dêg*" session embed messages on the difficulty of childbearing and the hardship parents go through to bring up children, thereby reminding the participants to be grateful to their parents and not to forget their roots. A number of shantangs also host columbaria within their premises where members can house urns and ancestral tablets of the deceased and it is not uncommon for generations of Teochews to be housed within one shantang, very similar to how they would have been buried within the same cemetery in the past.

Deity Worship

The Teochews, like many southern Chinese, practise deity worship or what is known commonly known as Taoism. Historical figures or personalities from folklore are revered for their virtues and other qualities, and they are deified by worshippers as a means of respect and also in the hope that these desirable qualities can be extended to them. Male deities are commonly referred to as "*Dua Lao Ia*" (大老爷). Temple festivals which include processions, religious ceremonies and opera performances are organised to celebrate the birthdays of these deities. "*ian lau'iâ*" (营老爷) is the Teochew term for the procession where the male deity is placed on a sedan chair and then hoisted and paraded by young men to the accompaniment of Teochew

An "*ngêng lau'iâ*" (营老爷) procession in Litang, Chao'an (潮安骊塘村)

"drum and cymbal" bands and other traditional performances. These processions together with the temple opera performances were often the highlight of the traditional festive calendar. Almost all the deities worshipped in Singapore and the associated rituals were brought over from similar practices in Chaozhou. Jonas Daniel Vaughan's *The Manners and Customs of the Chinese* published in 1879 observed that on "the 26th day of the 10th month of the lunar calendar the Tay Chews carry their idol in procession from their cemetery at Tanglin to their temple in Philip Street to see the theatricals held there in his honour". This practice of deity procession ended before World War II.

Chinese temples used to be divided along dialect lines but this boundary is almost non-existent today where worshippers from different dialect groups can be found within the same temple. Some deities historically worshipped by the Singapore Teochews are:

Mazu (妈祖): Born Lin Moniang (林默娘) in Meizhou (湄州), Fujian province in AD 960, she is said to have possessed supernatural power since she was young and had saved her fishermen father and brother from a sea storm. Mazu is the patron goddess revered by many Chinese living along coastal south China as she offers protection for people who are dependent on the sea for their living. Wak Hai Cheng Bio, the earliest known Teochew temple to be built in Singapore, was erected to honour her. In Singapore, Mazu temples are historically affiliated with early Chinese organizations as these temples served as the community hubs for early Chinese immigrants to obtain kinship support. Examples of such connections are Ngee Ann Kongsi and Wak Hai Cheng Bio for the Teochews, Hokkien Huay Kuan and Thian Hock Keng for the Hokkiens, Kiung Chow Hwee Kuan and Tin Hou Kong for the Hainanese, and Xing An Tian Hou Gong for the Heng Hua people.

For the many Teochews lived near water and depended on the seas for their livelihood, Mazu was even more important in providing the blessings needed to ensure their survival. This is evident in the number of Mazu temples erected by the Teochews in Singapore.In the 1930s, the Teochews in Kampong Tengah (present Sengkang), who were mostly fishermen, built a temple, Thian Hou Keng (半港天后宫). The temple moved to Pulau Ubin in 1980 before moving back to the mainland and joined with two other temples to be housed in a new building, the Sengkang Combined Temple, in 2001. Zhong Tou Gong (钟头宫) at Hougang Ave 5 was originally located in a fishing village in Hougang and moved to its current premises in 1985. Swatow Sia Mazu Temple (汕头社天后庙) in Geylang was set up in 1944 in Whampoa.

Xuan Tian Shang Di (玄天上帝): Also known as Xuan Wu Da Di (玄武大帝, Northern Emperor), Xuan Tian Shang Di represents the northern symbol in the Chinese constellation and is one of the higher-ranking Taoist deities. Due to his powerful ability to avert natural calamities, he was revered by the Ming emperors who built numerous temples in his honour, most notably in Wudangshan (武当山). Wak Hai Cheng Bio at Phillip Street is the earliest and most well-known Teochew temple in Singapore to worship him. He is also the resident deity in two other 19th century temples in Johor Bahru and Batam which are affiliated with the Teochews. His birthday falls on the 3rd day of the 3rd month in the lunar calendar.

Anji Shengwang (安济圣王): Anji Shengwang was originally named Wang Kang (王伉), an official during the Three Kingdoms period who died defending a city in Sichuan region and was worshipped by the people in Sichuan. A Teochew, Xie Shaocang (谢少苍), stationed in Sichuan during the Ming period brought a copy of his statue to Chaozhou. It was said that at the time of the statue's arrival, floods were raging in the Hanjiang (韩江) but it miraculously stopped when the statue was placed in the Qinglong Gumiao (青龙古庙, Green Dragon Temple) located on the riverbank. Grateful that Chaozhou city had been spared the flood calamity, the Teochews renamed Wang Kang as Anji Shengwang (安济圣王) or Lord of Peace and Salvation. An annual temple procession through the streets of the old Chaozhou city is held for him during the new lunar month.

In Singapore Anji Shengwang is primarily worshipped at the Ang Chee Sia Ong Temple, which traces its origin to 1918 when a Wang Dongqing (王东清) brought over the joss ash from the Green Dragon Temple in Chaozhou and set up a place of worship in his residence for his family and neighbours at Pasir Panjang 8th mile (杨桃园). In 1930, a proper temple was built at Pasir Panjang 7th mile and, in 1997, the temple moved to West Coast Drive.

Green Dragon Temple (青龙古庙) or Anji Wangmiao (安济王庙) where Anji Shengwang was first worshipped in Choazhou.

Festivals

Chinese New Year

Chinese New Year, which falls on the 1st day of the 1st month of the Chinese lunar calendar, is the most celebrated festival by Chinese worldwide. The importance of Chinese New Year and the first lunar month of a new year can be seen by the numerous practices and celebrations starting from the last lunar month of the preceding year until the 15th day of the 1st month of the new year. For the Teochews, preparation starts on the 24th day of the 12th lunar month with the "sending of the household god to heaven". On this day it is believed that the household god or "stove god" (灶神) ascends to Heaven to present his yearly report about the happenings in the household. Sumptuous food offerings are prepared for the deity with the most important being the "*loh teng zin*" (落汤钱), a sweet sticky delicacy made of glutinous rice flour coated with sweet peanut and sesame seeds bits, in the hope that a "sweet" report be presented to heaven. Also known as "Little New Year" (小过年), the day sees the Teochews busy cleaning up their homes and stocking up on household essentials, marking the start of the countdown towards the first day of the upcoming lunar new year.

On new year's eve, the Teochews put up couplets written with auspicious greetings on their doors and family members gather for the new year's eve reunion dinner called "surround the stove" or "*ui lou*" (围炉) to symbolise family unity. On the first day of the new year, the first act for the Teochews is to offer prayers to their ancestors and many would also observe a vegetarian diet on this day. Like all Chinese, the Teochews mark the occasion by donning new clothes, firing red firecrackers and, most importantly, visiting their elders, relatives and friends to give them their best wishes for the new year. The Teochews refer to this activity as "*pai zian*" (拜正) and greet one another with "*sing zian ru i*" (新正如意) because the first month of the lunar calendar is known as "*zian ghuêh*" (正月). Visitors to a Teochew household will be greeted with a plate of green olives and tangerines which symbolises "guests with auspicious visit" (宾临大吉). The olive is a replacement of the areca nut (槟榔)

Seu Teck Sean Tong conducting *pudu* prayer sessions.

family members. During this period the Teochew shantangs (善堂) would take the lead to organize the *pudu* (普渡) sessions to pray for universal salvation for all sentient beings.

Mid-Autumn Festival

The Mid-Autumn festival is celebrated on the 15th day of the 8th lunar month and because the moon appears to be at its biggest and brightest during this day, almost all practices associated with this festival revolves around the moon. An important part of the festive celebration is the worship of the moon goddess (拜月娘), conducted only by the womenfolk at home as the Teochews believe that "men don't worship the moon just as women don't make offerings to the kitchen god" (男不圆月，女不祭灶). The women involved have to be on a vegetarian diet for three days before the actual prayer day and only vegetarian items are allowed as offerings to the moon. The Teochews also pay their respects to their ancestors during this day and typical offerings include the "*la bian*" (朥饼), "*ze cêh go*" (书册糕), other Teochew confectionery and a "three meat" offering. "*La bian*" is a large pastry cake of about 8 inches (20 cm) in diameter with a sweet white "*dau sa*" filling made of mung bean. "*La*" (朥) is lard in the Teochew dialect and the traditional recipe calls for the use of lard in both the rich flaky pastry and the filling. A Teochew folk tale tells of the cruelty of the Mongol or "Hu" soldiers when they invaded and occupied Chaozhou, and in response, the Teochews started the practice of using yam as an offering because in the Teochew dialect yam (芋头) is pronounced "*ou tau*", similar to "*ou tau*" (胡头, the "head of the Hu person"). After the prayers, family members would gather outside the house to enjoy the confectionery and tea under the bright full moon.

Moon worship or "*bai ghuêh niên*" (拜月娘) session at a Chaoshan household during the Mid-Autumn Festival.

Double Nine Festival

The other festival in autumn is the "Double Nine Festival" (重阳节) so named because it falls on the 9th day of the 9th lunar month and is marked by kite-flying and hiking. During this period, the weather is cool and windy and hence suitable for flying kites. In parts of the Chaoshan region, people believe that the occasion offers an opportunity to change their fortune and flying the kites high and letting them go symbolises the release of bad luck. Hiking and soaking up the autumn atmosphere was a revered activity of the literati in the past and many famous Chinese poets were known

"Iu mua uêng" (油麻员), a confectionery distributed to friends and relatives for goodwill during the Double Nine Festival and also used as an offering to the Nine Emperor Gods.

to have composed poems commemorating the occasion. The Teochew specialty food item for this festival is the "*iu mua uêng*" (油麻员), a deep fried confectionery item made of glutinous rice and sesame oil and mixed with crushed peanuts. This is given to relatives, friends and neighbours as a sign of goodwill or *jieyuan* (结缘) because the character "*uêng*" (员) is a homophone of "*uêng*" (缘, relationship) in the Teochew dialect. A related event is the the nine days Nine Emperor Gods Festival starting from the 1st day of the month and popularly celebrated by Teochews.

Winter Solstice

The last seasonal festival is the "*Dang Zoih*" (冬节, Winter Solstice) which usually falls on the 21st or 22nd of December. During this day "*diem in*" (甜圆), balls of glutinous rice flour cooked in a sweet soup, is consumed as the sticky rice balls and sweet soup symbolise family unity. The Teochews also visit their ancestors' graves and perform similar rituals as on Tomb Sweeping Day. The act is known as "*guê dang zua*" (过冬纸) because it is carried out in winter. Offerings include tea, wine, meat from three types of livestock, Teochew kuehs, fruits and cooked cockles. Like the Qingming festival, the cockles are consumed on the spot and the shells are used to hold down the paper strips to symbolise leaving money for the ancestors.

Rites of Passage

The Teochews have customs for all aspects of one's life covering birth, coming of age, marriage and death. There are many variants to these customs across districts, towns and even villages, and only the most commonly-practised rituals are briefly discussed here. Many of these customs are no longer practised by the Teochews in the Chaoshan region and overseas.

Birth

When a woman becomes pregnant, her maternal family has to prepare gifts of meat and eggs as nourishment and well wishes for her. During this time, she would avoid travelling, sewing, dyeing, nailing and any form of ground-breaking activity. This gestational period is known as the *cuisheng li* (催生礼). After the baby is born the first twelve or thirty days of birth is known as the *jilaqi* (忌腊期) or confinement period and precautions are taken to ensure the well-being of the baby and mother during this period. Both are to be kept in a quiet room free of disturbance from humans or animals, and the mother would observe a vegetarian diet . On a baby's third day, he or she would be bathed in water containing Chinese mugwort (艾叶), pomelo leaves and ginger in a ritual known as *xisanzhao* (洗三朝), followed by a celebration meal to which the midwife and the family's elderly folks would be invited. If a boy is born, a red note written with the child's eight birth characters (year, month, day and time of birth) is sent to the woman's maternal family together with pomegranate flowers (榴花) and sweet confectionary. On the 12th day, the baby's maternal grandparents would then send a maternal grandson congratulatory gift (办外孙) which consists of four tangerines, sugared bean strips, a cooked rooster, a piece of pork belly and 12 red-coloured eggs. However, only a small portion of the gift is kept by the baby's paternal family who would then prepare additional items to be offered together

Shop in Chaozhou city specializing in ceremony items associated with the Teochew rites of passage.

Cleansing and Clothing of the Deceased (沐浴更衣): At the death of an old man his body will be cleansed with water boiled in herbs. He is then dressed in the funeral clothes. A lamp is lit at the deceased's feet or head to "provide him direction". A bowl of rice for the deceased's comsumption in the afterworld is also placed beside the lamp.

Hanging the Mourning Curtain (挂孝帘): A white banner is placed over the door of the home together with white lanterns and a white couplet in blue ink to indicate that a death has occurred in the family.

Death Notification (发讣告): Friends and relatives are notified of the death either by word of mouth or through placing an obituary notice in the newspaper.

Donning of Mourning Garments (赐杖成服): The deceased's family members will don mourning garments which include head gear, clothes and special shoes. In the past, mourning sticks were also given to support the grieving family. Garments are marked in different colours to represent the mourners' relationships with the deceased.

Informing the Earth Deity (报地头): In the past, when an old man died in the family, his sons and grandsons would proceed to the local earth god temple to report the death.

Setting up the Wake (设灵堂): The wake is set up to allow friends and relatives to pay their last respects to the deceased. It can be at the home of the deceased or in funeral parlours which are decked in blue banners. Paper offerings to be used for the deceased's afterlife are also placed in the hall.

Feeding the Dead (饲生、恋亲视尸): Once the wake is set up, the mourning son would kneel in front of the deceased with a bowl of rice, a plate of dried beancurd and brown sugar and then proceed to use one end of the chopsticks to put food in the deceased's mouth and the other end to feed himself. This ritual symbolises the son's acknowledgement of his parent's efforts in bringing him up, and he shows his gratitude by sending the parent off. The use of two end of the chopsticks represents that both parties are forever separated. After this ritual, the priest will walk around the body chanting prayers, followed by the family members in order of seniority.

"Coffining" (接棺、入殓): After the body is placed in the coffin, joss money, tea leaves and other burial items are scattered around the body. Once all the descendants are present, the coffin is nailed in with auspicious words uttered with each nail. Coffins for males are red while those for females are black.

Paying Respects (吊唁): The funeral wake is held for relatives and friends to pay their respects to the deceased. It ranges in duration from three to seven days and is always held for an odd number of days because even numbers are associated with joyous occasions. On arrival, the visitor approaches the altar placed in front of the coffin, lights a single joss-stick and bows to the deceased as a mark of respect. As the "host", one or more representatives of the deceased's family will stand or kneel by the side of the altar and bow to the visitor to acknowledge the paying of respects. The visitor will also bow to the "host" before leaving the altar.

Keeping Vigil (守灵): The deceased's family is expected to keep vigil all day and night at the wake.

Releasing the Soul from Purgatory (超度): Sometimes known as "*gong dêg*" (功德) in the Teochew dialect, prayers are conducted for the deceased according to either Buddhist or Taoist rites or a combination of both.

Funeral (出殡、安葬): The funeral procession is led by a family elder who will toss joss money to "buy the way". This is followed by the condolence banners and streamers, the coffin which is hoisted by eight men or carried in a hearse flanked by immediate family members, a band of musicians playing drum and gong music and, finally, respectful friends and relatives. In the past, the family members would walk the deceased all way to the cemetery. At the grave, the priest will chant prayers, after which the sons will throw grain seeds into the grave before the coffin is lowered and the grave sealed.

End of Mourning (脱孝): The household and the family members remove all signs of mourning. This can only be done after the "gong dêg" session is completed.

Ancestor Enactment (点主、升龛): After three months or 100 days, the deceased is installed as an ancestor. An ancestral tablet is made and placed either at home, a temple or the clan ancestral hall.

CUISINE & TEA CULTURE

Cuisine

The conventional categorisation of Han Chinese cuisine based on historical provincial boundaries broadly breaks it into eight main categories: Lu cuisine (鲁菜) from Shandong, Hui cuisine (徽菜) from Anhui, Canton cuisine (粤菜) from Guangdong, Min cuisine (闽菜) from Fujian, Xiang cuisine (湘菜) from Hunan, Huaiyang cuisine (淮扬菜) from Jiangsu, Szechuan cuisine (川菜) from Sichuan and Zhe cuisine (浙菜) from Zhejiang. As Chaozhou had historically existed as a prefecture under the Guangdong province, Teochew cuisine is clubbed together with Cantonese cuisine under the umbrella "Yue" or Canton cuisine despite being quite different from Cantonese cuisine in terms of its cooking styles and its use of ingredients, seasonings and condiments. In places like Singapore and Hong Kong where there is a significant population representation from the two dialect groups, Cantonese and Teochew cuisines are recognised as separate cuisines with restaurants specialising in each cuisine. This differentiation is not a recent phenomenon in Singapore. A 19th century Jiangxi merchant Pan Naiguang (潘乃光) who travelled extensively in Southeast Asia wrote more than 100 poems in 1895 describing the sights encoutered on his travels. In one of the passages related to Chinese restaurants in Singapore he mentioned that "Cantonese and Teochew cuisines were equal in representation operating in the Chinese restaurant business" (买醉相邀上酒楼，唐人不与老番侔。开厅点菜须庖宰，半是潮州半广州).

The Teochew palate can be simply described as one that is heavy on seafood but light on seasoning, a love for sweetness coupled with a penchant for pickled products, and an emphasis on a delicate cooking style that borders on minimalism to preserve the clean natural flavours of food. The cuisine is synonymous with fresh ingredients, subtle seasoning and light cooking methods.

Culinary Principles

The Chaoshan region's proximity to the sea and rivers and the presence of good agricultural land and a tropical climate allow for cultivation almost all year round, providing its people access to fresh aquatic and land produce on a regular basis. Because of this availability of fresh ingredients, the Teochews have an appreciation for the natural taste of food and have developed a cuisine that values seasonality of ingredients paired with a culinary principle that food should retain as much of its natural flavour as possible. To the Teochews, ingredients used must be "*cin*" (鲜, fresh) and in flavouring, the emphasis is on "*ceng*" (清, subtlety in taste) based on a belief that a light touch brings out the best in food. Hence

sorts of vegetables and seafood. There are generally three categories of "*zab giem*". The first comprises the classic vegetable pickles where greens and roots are immersed in brine or vinegar. Examples of this category are the Teochew salted vegetable "*giem cai*" (咸菜) made from mustard green (大芥菜) and "*cai pou*" (菜脯) made from radish. The second category comprises "marinated pickles" (酱菜) which involve marinating vegetables in mixtures based on soy sauce or savoury bean pastes or oil. The third type is the curing of seafood either into a dried form like the salted fish or immersing items such as small crabs and shellfish in soy sauce combined with chilli, garlic, vinegar or liquor. Some of these "*zab giem*" items are also used with other ingredients during food preparation. For example, "*gan na cai*" (橄榄菜) is used to create olive fried rice and "*giem cai*" is used during the preparation of steamed fish or duck soup.

So important are the pickles to the Teochews that they even followed the footsteps of the Teochew immigrants to their overseas destinations. The export of Chaozhou salted vegetables, mostly to Southeast Asia, more than doubled from 46,000 piculs (2,760 tonnes) in 1870 to 93,000 piculs (5,580 tonnes) in 1890 to 224,000 piculs (13,440 tonnes) in 1910, mirroring the trend of Teochew overseas migration.

The Teochews are also known for their use of rice flour to produce a large variety of Teochew kuehs (粿) and a rice noodle more commonly known as kway teow in Southeast Asia. Like "*mue*", kway teow is an indispensable part of the Teochew culinary make-up and it forms the basis of many popular hawker foods like fried kway teow, beef kway teow and fishball kway teow. Another rendition of the kway teow rice noodle is combined with another Teochew classic, the braised meat to create "kway chap" (粿汁), a popular hawker food where braised pork and pig innards are consumed with the rice noodles immersed in braised gravy. A popular phrase "Teochew kway teow Hokkien mee, Hylam kopi Canton chow" (潮州粿条福建面，海南咪呸广府炒) used in early Singapore and Malaya aptly sums up the culinary identity of the various Chinese dialect groups in this region and highlights the association of kway teow with the Teochews. It is no coincidence that any place with a Teochew diaspora such as Thailand and Vietnam would include kway teow–based dishes in their local cuisine.

Kuehs and Confectionery

Teochew kuehs originated as celebration fare and as forms of offerings to deities and ancestors, and each occasion or festival would have its own types of kueh offerings (时节做时粿). For example, "*ce keg guê*" (鼠曲粿) is made for the Chinese New Year period. On the 15th day of the Chinese New Year, three other types of kuehs are made: the sweet rice cake "*tiam guê*"(甜粿), to symbolise the sweetness of life; steamed rice cake "huek guê" (发粿), for fortune; and carrot cake (菜头粿), for good luck. The white "*pêh to guê*" (白桃粿) is made as an offering to the dead during the 7th lunar month and the white sweet flat "moon" cake "*guêh guê*" (月糕) is offered at moon worship during the Mid-Autumn Festival. Kueh preparation is a time-consuming affair which requires patience and dedication. Preparing and offering kuehs to the gods and ancestors represents the Teochews' respect and sincerity, and kueh consumption after the kuehs have been offered is a means of connecting with the revered. Today, the making and consumption of Teochew kuehs are no longer limited to the festivals and seasons.

Traditional wooden Teochew kueh moulds. Kueh-making taps into the Teochew wood-carving art form to turn food offerings into objects of beauty.

Kueh-making is traditionally the purview of the womenfolk and in the past a woman skilful in the art of kueh-making was perceived to be a desirable wife. A large variety of kuehs are created through a permutation of the dough ingredients (rice flour, sweet potato flour, wheat flour or sweet potato), the flavouring or colouring ingredients (herbs or seasonings), the use of leavened or unleavened dough, the types of savoury or sweet fillings, and the shape and size the kuehs take. Many classic Teochew kuehs are shaped in intricately carved wooden moulds resulting in the rendition of exquisitely patterned kuehs, a reflection of the Teochews' penchant for beauty and details.

Teochew confectionery consists of different "*bian*" (饼, pastry), "*teng*" (糖, sweets) and "*go*" (糕, rice flour cakes). These cover a wide variety of pastry items with sweet and savoury fillings, cookies, sweetened rice flour products and candied items. Like Teochew kuehs, these items are not only snacks but are also food items used to mark different occasions and festivals in addition to being used as offerings. The quintessential Teochew flaky pastry is traditionally made with lard as reflected in the name of its most representative item the "*a piàn*" (朥饼), which literally translates into "lard pastry". Over the years vegetable oil is used in place of lard by most of the Teochew confectionary makers in Singapore.

A Teochew "char kway teow" stall at night market in Singapore (1965)

Versatility

Given the Chaoshan region's proximity to other sub-ethnic cultures and its people's history with immigration, the Teochews have long been influenced by the culinary practices of other cultures. Teochew beef kway teow is a marriage of the Hakka beef consumption habit with the Teochew staple kway teow and the food item spread to various part of Southeast Asia with Teochew immigrants. Satay sauce from the Malay cuisine was adapted by Teochews in Singapore as the gravy used in satay bee hoon, a hawker dish made up of bee hoon (rice vermicelli) topped with pork, liver, kang kong (water spinach), dry bean curd and clams. The same Malay sauce was also brought back to the Chaoshan region by returning Teochews to create Shacha sauce (沙茶酱), a Chaoshan condiment popularly used in China. Many hawker food items in Singapore such as Teochew minced pork noodles and bah-kut-teh are results of the influence from other Chinese and non-Chinese groups as well as the adoption of locally available ingredients.

Today there exists three schools of Teochew restaurants: the "authentic" Chaoshan style, the Hong Kong style and the "Nanyang" or Southeast Asia style. The Hong Kong school is known for its use of high-end quality ingredients sourced from all over the world while the "Nanyang" school is recognized for both its adaptation to local conditions and its ability to preserve traditional Teochew dishes lost in China. Despite the differentiation, Teochews everywhere continue to adhere to the principles of fresh ingredients, skills and subtle seasoning in their food preparation and consumption.

From affordable hawker fare to high-end restaurant delicacies, from daily meals served at home to festive offerings made for gods and ancestors, from delicate confectionery morsels to multiple courses in lavish banquets, the Teochews have created a culinary repertoire covering every occasion in their lives. To the Teochews, food preparation is not merely to fill one's stomach but is an integral part of their culture to be carried out with dedication and finesse, just like what they do for all their other art forms and cultural pursuits.

teapot for tea brewing. The gai'ou is a three-piece set of tea ware consisting of a lid, a cup or bowl and a saucer. This practice of using the gai'ou is to cater to the brewing of the Dancong tea because its tea leaves are larger and fit better in this vessel compared to the teapot. Another recognizable feature of "*ganghu tê*" is the presence of just three teacups to form the Chinese character *pin* (品) for "appreciate". If there are more than three drinkers, then the emptied teacups are rinsed with hot water before they are rotated to the other drinkers. A popular Teochew phrase "three for tea, four for drinks and two to travel" (茶三酒四踢跎二) alludes to the use of three teacups in the tea ware setting for "*ganghu tê*".

While the Teochews were not the first to consume tea nor are they the only people who practise "*ganghu tê*", they stand out in the extent to which they have integrated tea culture into their lives. In many places, any form of tea culture is reserved for special occasions and in some cases is even treated as a ceremony, but for the Teochews the tea culture is their daily ritual. In the Chaoshan region, more Oolong tea is consumed than water and the tea consumed is always freshly brewed with tea leaves because it is unacceptable to use tea bags or consume tea that was prepared hours before. The same tea preparation process is repeated whenever tea is called for, and tea sets are found everywhere in homes, offices, eateries, stores and even roadside hawker stalls. One cannot walk into a Chaoshan household or talk business with a Chaoshan company without having a round of "*ganghu tê*". The tea culture is so prevalent in the Chaoshan region that stores selling tea and tea ware are common sights while tea houses are almost non-existent. It is also said that the Chaoshan region's tea consumption per capital is the highest in China.

"*Ganghu tê*" is less prevalent in the Singapore Teochew community today but one visible sign of its presence in Singapore culinary culture is in the local dish the Teochew bah-kut-teh. Bah -kut-teh's creation is linked to the early Teochew immigrants working along the Singapore River who tapped their access to pepper and pork bones to create a peppery pork-based broth. Teochews would wash down the oil from the broth with a brew of "*ganghu tê*" and this practice is still found in the many bah kut teh eateries today.

Tea consumption in a coffeshop on Cumming Street, Singapore (1980). Cumming Street is located within the Ellenborough Market area dominated by Teochews. In this coffeeshop the brazier, kettle and tea set were placed on each table and the patron would just order and pay for the tea leaves.

including polychrome painting (彩绘), gold powder painting (擂金画), porcelain chard sculptures (嵌瓷), clay friezes (泥塑), wood carvings (木雕) and stone carvings (石雕) are employed on the roof, gable ends, walls, beams, brackets, columns and doors. The ornamentation can be categorized into three groups, namely human figures, elements of nature and geometric motive, and the stories and expressions associated with these ornaments reflect the owner's aspiration and desire for himself and his descendants. Human figures are inspired by characters from popular operas and folklores and are chosen to advocate desired values such as loyalty (忠), filial piety (孝), humanity (仁), integrity (节) and righteousness (义). Aspiration of abundance, happiness, longevity and procreation are often conveyed through the various representation of flora and fauna, creatures of land and sea and geometric motives which play on the monosyllabic nature of the Chinese language and its multitude of words sharing similar pronunciation to manipulate ideas, ideographs and pictures.

Front of Seah Eu Chin's residence at North Boat Quay.

Four Grand Residences

Song Ong Siang in his 1923 book *One Hundred Years of the Chinese in Singapore* made reference to the houses of four prominment merchants, namely Tan Seng Poh, Seah Cheo Seah, Wee Ah Hood and Tan Yeok Nee, as the "four residences built in typical Chinese architectural design and style". As these four merchants were Teochews, their residences were collectively nicknamed the "Four Grand Residences" (四大厝) by latter generations.

The first of the four residences to be built was Tan Seng Poh's in 1869, located at 58 Hill Street at the junction withth Loke Yew Street. Tan Seng Poh was born in Ipoh, the son of Tan Ah Hun, the Kapitan Cina of Perak. He moved to Singapore at the age of nine following the marriage of his sister to Seah Eu Chin and later made his fortune through the opium trade. In 1871 he became the first Chinese to serve as a Municipal Commissioner and was made a Justice of Peace in 1872. Seng Poh Road and Seng Poh Lane in Tiong Bahru estate are named after him. Tan Seng Poh's residence also served as the office of *Zuo Binglong* (左秉隆), the first official Chinese Consul to Singapore appointed by the Qing government in 1881. After Tan Seng Poh's death in 1879 the house was put up for auction in November 1900 and later demolished and replaced by a row of shophouses by 1904. While there is no known surviving photograph of the house, it was described in an 1895 newspaper article as being "built after the Chinese mansion style and it is a desirable residence for a well-to-do Chinaman".

Seah Eu Chin's residence at 11 North Boat Quay was built in 1872 by his son Seah Cheo Seah who, like his father, was also a Justice of the Peace. The residence was described to "have possessed a grand Teochew-style entrance gate, three courtyards and two double-storey houses" with its entrance at North Boat Quay facing the Singapore River and its rear on High Street. Seah Eu Chin was born in Yuebu village (澄海月浦) of the Chenghai county in 1805 and came to Singapore in 1823. He worked as a clerk aboard several trading ships and by 1830 had established a successful trading firm, but it was his venture in the cultivation and trading of gambier where he amassed a vast fortune. His stature as a community leader saw him leading the Singapore Chinese community in welcoming Lord Dalhousie, Governor General of India, during his visit to Singapore in 1850. Seah Eu Chin was appointed Grand Juror from 1851 and was made a Justice of the Peace in 1867. His influence within the Chinese community enabled him to mediate in numerous disputes, most notably during the Hokkien Teochew Riot of 1854. He died in the North Boat Quay residence in 1883 and the house was demolished after World War II and Guthrie & Company built a godown on the location. The premises are now part of the Singapore Parliament House compound.

Wee Ah Hood's two-storey house at 49 Hill Street was built in 1878 and is also known as *Dafudi* (大夫第, "Imperial Official's Residence"). Wee Ah Hood's father, Wee Ah Heng, had settled in Malacca by 1810, but died at age 32 when Wee Ah Hood was six months old Wee Ah Hood was born in Circular Road in 1828 and made his fortune in the textile as well as the gambier and pepper trade After his death in 1875 his son Wee Kim Yam, an active Chinese community leader, leased out the building to numerous parties including the St Mary's Home from 1900 to 1905. In 1906, the General Chinese Trade Affairs Association (later Singapore Chinese Chamber of Commerce) moved into the building shortly after its inaugural meeting at the Thong Chai Medical Institution. The Chamber initially leased the premises but bought over it in 1908, and it was renumberd to 47 Hill Street in the 1920s. In 1939 Tan Lark Sye with the support of the Chamber's President Lee Kong Chian proposed to erect a five-storey building on the site but the plan was halted by the outbreak of World War II. After the war, there were a few attempts at reconstruction, and in 1963, the original residence structure was replaced with a new building.

House of Wee Ah Hood at Hill Street c 1950s.

Nanyang Sacred Union at River Valley Road (2015).

Both Seah Eu Chin's and Wee Ah Hood's residences point to a courtyard mansion style made up of a hybrid of Chaozhou and Straits Settlements architectural styles. They were characterised by a traditional Teochew ornate entrance gate opening into a foreyard while the building structure itself is made up of the "five-foot-way" storeyed shophouses instead of any Chaozhou dwelling typology. Another similar building of this design, albeit of a smaller scale, exists today in the premises of the Nanyang Sacred Union at River Valley Road. Nanyang Sacred Union occupies three houses — 251, 253 and 255 River Valley Road, and house number 253 used to be the townhouse of Seah Song Seah, the third son of Seah Eu Chin.

PERFORMING ARTS

Opera

The most well-known and well-loved performing arts for the Teochews is the Teochew opera. An old art form which has its origin in *nanxi* (南戏, "Southern Opera"), it was known as *chaodiao* (潮调, "Chaozhou tune") during the Ming period. The Qing dynasty witnessed increased popularity and many of the current forms of the Teochew opera such as its scripts, training system, performing methods were developed during this period.

Characteristics

Like all Chinese opera, Teochew opera is a multi-disciplinary theatrical genre that tells a story through singing, speech, movements, instrumental accompaniment and stage props.

The traditional opera troupe was organised with different roles including administrators, instructor or choreographer, performers, musicians, backstage and theatre owner. A small- to medium-sized troupe would typically engage at least 80 people and bigger troupes were operating with more than 100 people each. In addition to ticketed performances staged in the local theatres, many troupes were engaged to perform in other parts in Southeast Asia, Hong Kong and even China. Similar to other Chinese opera genre, Teochew opera also uses a role type (角色) system to establish the various roles. There were as many as seven roles in the initial period, but today the major roles are *sheng* (生, male), *dan* (旦, female), *chou* (丑, comic) and *jing* (净, valiant), with the comic role being the most recognizable feature of the Teochew opera genre.

One feature of the traditional Teochew opera troupe was the presence of child performers (童伶) whose voices were deemed most suitable for achieving the tonal and pitch requirements of Teochew opera singing. These young children were usually from poor families, and bonded by their parents to the troupes for an average period of seven years. During this period, they received strict training under harsh supervision, with punishment often meted out for disobedience and poor performance. The colonial government in Singapore determined that the training regimen and treatment of child performers was inhumane and sought to protect child performers through legislation such as the Children Ordinance (1927) and the Children and Young Persons Act (1933). In an attempt to continue Teochew opera's performing tradition, leaders from the Poit Ip Huay Kuan intervened and undertook the responsibility to look after the welfare of the child performers. One anecdote relates that as part of an agreement to appease the colonial government, Teochew community leaders such as Yeo Chan Boon, Lee Wee Nam, Lee Kim Soo and Lim

Kim Seng took turns to attend opera performances almost nightly to supervise and ensure the well-being of the performing children. The Children and Young Persons Ordinance (1949) enforced on 1 Aug 1950 made it unlawful for anyone under the age of 17 to take part in any public performance without the permission of the Commission of Labour, putting a gradual end to the practice in Singapore.

The music of Teochew opera is based on a combination of string-of-tune "medley" (联曲体) and tempo-variant form (板腔体). Teochew opera music adopts the same four modal systems as other Chaozhou music to reflect emotions of light-heartedness, outburst, humour and melancholy. A trait of Teochew opera's vocal style is the bangsheng (帮声, "assisting voice") in which multiple voices emphasise certain parts of a solo tune in unison, usually at the end of a phrase.

The accompanying instrumental ensemble for Teochew opera comprises the "*bhu puêng*" (武畔, "military section") and the "*bhung puêng*" (文畔,"civil section"), with the military section on stage left and the civil section on stage right. The civil section consists of woodwind instruments including the *erxian* (二弦, two-stringed bowed fiddle), *yehu* (椰胡, "coconut" fiddle), *suona* (唢呐) and *yangqin* (扬琴, hammered dulcimer). The erxian is the lead instrument known as the *touxian* (头弦) and its player is acknowledged as the lead player as he directs the civil section. The lead player's playing position is a unique feature of classical Chaozhou music performance: he sits cross-legged with the instrument's soundbox on his left thigh which he supports with the ball of his right foot. From his position, he has a good view of the entire civil section and the opera performance area to his left. The yehu supports the erxian usually through doubling at a lower octave and is therefore also known as the "secondary fiddle". It is not uncommon for the civil section to have only three musicians: a lead player who plays both the erxian and suona, and one player each on the yangqin and yehu. The military section is made up of the large and small drums (大鼓小鼓), large and small cymbals (大钹小钹), *ban* (板, wooden clappers), *bangzi* (梆子, woodblock), *qinzi* (钦仔, "small knobbed gong"), *quluo* (曲锣, "tune" gong) and the "deep wave" *shenbo* (深钹, large gongs). The leader of the miliary section plays the ban, xiaogu, and bangzi and sits facing the other percussionists with a full view of the performance on his right. Two musicians play the shenbo and quluo suspended from a horizontal pole, and one alternates between the handheld qinzi and bo.

Child Performers (童伶). A Teochew saying "Only the spineless parents would sell their children into acting" (父母无修世，卖仔去做戏) highlights the plight of these young performers sold into bondage with the opera troupes.

History

Jonas Daniel Vaughan, one of Singapore's longest-residing Europeans, noted in 1879 that "theatricals" were held in the "Tay Chew" temple at Phillip Street. Li Zhongjue (李钟珏) also mentioned the presence of

Teochew street opera performance by Sin Yong Wah Heng (新荣和兴) at North Boat Quay (1980).

were also known as "*zua ian bang*" (纸影班), the same name given to Teochew puppetry troupes because many members of the puppetry troupes also took up "*cêng ciang*" engagements. In "walk singing", a small group of performers which can comprise just two singers, a percussionist and a string player would move around from business to business in public places such as shops and market stalls especially during the Chinese New Year period. Stall holders would then give the group ang-pows or red packets as token of appreciation for their performance.

Puppetry

Teochew metal rod puppetry (铁枝木偶) is widely known as "*zua ian hi*" (纸影戏, "shadow puppetry") to the Teochews. Its name is a reflection of the craft's origin in Minnan shadow puppetry which came to Chaozhou in the Ming period. During the Qing period, the two-dimensional leather-cut figure of Minnan shadow puppetry was replaced with a three-dimensional puppet that had a straw torso, paper hands, wooden legs and a clay head moulded in a style similar to a Chaozhou Dawu clay figurine. Clothed in opera costume, the puppet had three rods attached for manipulation, one to each hand and another for the puppet's back. The paper screen was also replaced with a glass screen and puppeteers later substituted a backdrop for the glass screen. Simple props such as chairs and tables were used on the stage . As the puppets were manipulated in the same manner as in the original shadow puppetry, Teochews continue to refer to the craft as "shadow puppetry" and puppetry troupes are known as "*zua ian bang*" (纸影班, "shadow puppet troupe"). With singing, music and scripts similar to Teochew opera, a puppetry performance was akin to a "micro opera". Opera singers and musicians were also known to cross over to puppetry performances and some opera troupes were known to operate both puppetry and opera performances at the time .

There is no known record of when Teochew puppetry was first performed Singapore. From a 2012 interview with *Wu Yarong* (吴亚荣), the 76-year-old owner of Teochew puppetry troupe Sin Sai Poh Hong (新赛宝丰) who inherited the troupe from his father claimed that Sin Sai Poh Hong was approximately 100 years old. Like Teochew opera, Teochew puppetry performances are put on as part of festive activities in the temples. A typical puppetry performance requires at least 12 performers including the puppeteers, singers and musicians. The puppeteers and singers are not the same people and, like Teochew opera, the musicians are also divided into civil and military sections. In Singapore the term "*zua ian bang*" was extended to refer to professional music troupes consisting of only singers and musicians. A likely reason is that the singers and musicians from the puppetry troupes were often engaged to perform without the puppetry shows and, over time, the popularity of such engagements led to the formation of music-only troupes who adopted the same term "*zua ian bang*" as the puppetry troupes. Unlike puppetry troupes, these musical "*zua ian bangs*" were seldom engaged to perform for religious events. Instead, they were often engaged by clan associations and businesses to provide entertainment during organisational events or festive occasions. Wealthier Teochew families were also known to engage "*zua ian bang*" to perform during family celebrations such as coming-of-age ceremonies, birthdays and weddings.

The golden age for Teochew puppetry was during the 1940s when a temple might host two or three performances at the same time. The busiest engagement period was the 3rd lunar month which coincided with several deities' birthdays and the 7th lunar month of the Hungry Ghost Festival. The former would usually involve the entire puppetry troupe while the latter would involve just the singers or the singers and musicians. For Sin Sai Poh Hong, the peak of the art form was reached in the 1970s when the troupe had more than a dozen days of engagement per month, but this declined in the 1980s and, since the 2000s, it has been reduced to a dozen engagements per year. The troupe has also moved from hiring full-timers to part-timers. Sin Sai Poh Hong staged its last performance in September 2015, leaving Sin Ee Lye Heng (新怡梨兴) as the sole surviving troupe in Singapore performing Teochew metal rod puppetry.

Teochew music records produced by Er Woo Amateur Dramatic Association and Tseng Tseng Musical Association (铮铮丝竹社). The latter is an association formed by prominent Teochew music practitioners to share and promote Chinese music.

emphasis on the left-hand vibrating technique over the right-hand plucking. Known as "one sound many tones" (一音多韵), detailed vibration is applied by the left hand to one pluck by the right hand.

The Chaoyang wind music (潮阳笛套) has its origin in court music and is a popular style in Chaoyang and Shantou where the lead instruments are wind instruments and can be accompanied by either string instruments or percussion instruments. The primary instruments are the flute, guan (管, double-reed pipe), sheng (笙, free reed mouth organ) and *dongxiao* and the secondary string instruments are *sanxian*, *pipa* and zheng as well as percussion instruments like drums, cymbals and gongs.

Temple Music

Teochew temple music evolved from selected tunes from Buddhist prayer chants and is performed primarily by wind and percussion instruments. The performance style and content can vary from temple to temple. In Singapore, this type of music is mostly associated with the shantangs (善堂) which have their own resident music departments to support the performance of this music. There are two main styles of Teochew temple music: the Chanhe (禅和, "Zen Harmony") and the Xianghua (香花, "Incense Flower").

One theory attributes the Chanhe style's introduction into Chaozhou to abbot Venerable *Mi Yin* (密因) during the Qing dynasty when he was appointed the abbot of Kai Yuan Temple in Chaozhou city in 1736. Another theory attributes its creation to the efforts of secular Buddhist follower *Qiu Jiaxiang* (邱家祥) and the monks of Kai Yuan Temple. Nevertheless, the Chanhe style is distinctively Teochew in terms of its music mode and instruments used. The repertoire comprises hymns based on the Yogacara Flaming Mouth Ceremony of Yun Qi, or composed out of various Buddhist texts. The hymns are sung mainly in Classical Chinese with some sinicised Sanskrit words to the accompanied of Chaozhou instruments such as the suona, yangqin, pipa, xiaosanxian and yehu. Other instruments such as cymbals, muyu (木鱼，wooden fish), bells, chimes and gongs are also played along with the music and a drummer controls the rhythm and tempo of the entire chant.

The Xianghua style was practised in Chaozhou before the introduction of the Chanhe style from Kai Yuan Temple and is perceived by some to be the incumbent form of Buddhist music in Chaozhou. As the Xianghua style's rhythm and tone resemble Buddhist hymns in Zhangzhou and Quanzhou and it also contains elements from Southern Min opera, it is believed to have been transmitted from Fujian to Chaozhou. The music repertoire consists of more than 100 pieces, many of which derive from Buddhist and Taoist hymns of the various Chaozhou regions. These hymns are sung with the accompaniment of the same Teochew music instruments.

Drum Music

Teochew drum music comprises percussion instruments including the large drum (大锣鼓), small drum (小锣鼓), Su drum (苏锣鼓) and gongs and cymbals. The most representative rendition of Teochew drum music is the Teochew "gong and drum" music (潮州大锣鼓) which is arguably the music genre most associated with Teochews. It is primarily a large-scale percussion-based public music performance format led by the suonas. When Han Yu was in Chaozhou, he noted that percussion and wind instruments were used during religious rites, and by the Yuan dynasty, these instruments had evolved

w music lovers “jamming” at a temple in the Ellenborough Market or Sin Pa Sat area (1970s). Playing music with like-minded individuals is a common pastime among Teochew men. (c.1970s)

Selection of Localised Words in Singapore Teochew Dialect

	Pronunciation	Meaning	Possible Sources	Source Word
土豆	tou dao	groundnut	Localised	ground nut
镭	lui	money	Localised	
盾囝	dung gian	coin	Localised	
霜橱	seng du	refrigerator	Localised	“frost cupboard”
绑柔	bang riu	handkerchief	Localised	
肩头	goin tau	shoulder	Localised	
花猫白舌	hue ngieu beh zih	sweet lie	Localised	
骗人	piang nang	deceptive	Localised	
讨厌	to iam	irritating	Localised	
附近	hu geng	nearby	Localised	
差错	ca co	mistake	Localised	
潦草	lo co	scrawl	Localised	
要紧	iao ging	important	Localised	
袅使、得	boi sai/dig	cannot	Localised	
真	zing	truly, really	Hokkien	
逐摆	dah bai	every time	Hokkien	
淡薄	dam boh	a little	Hokkien	
歹势	dai sê	to be embarrassed by	Hokkien	
巴刹	ba sag	market	Malay	pasar
大比	dab bi	but	Malay	tetapi
交寅	gau ing	marry	Malay	kahwin
干筒	gang tang	potato	Malay	kentang
沙中	sua dong	cuttlefish	Malay	sotong
老君	lau gung	doctor	English	locum (physician)
老君厝	lau gung cu	hospital	English+Teochew	locum+cu

	Pronunciation	Meaning	Possible Sources	Source Word
砂喇	sa la	wrong	Malay	salah
砂阳	sa iang	pamper	Malay	sayang
砂央	sa iang	a pity	Malay	sayang
打汉	ta hang	tolerate	Malay	tahan
巴仙 / 仆升	ba sieng	percent	English	percent
塞文	sag bhung	soap	Portugese	sabun
胶薄(棉)	ga boh (mi)	silk cotton	Malay	kapok
菠薐	puê lêng	spinach	Historical	translated from ancient name of Nepal (菠薐国)
甲必	gah big	suitcase	English	case bag
咖哩	gia li	curry	English	curry
士巴拿	se ba na	spanner	English	spanner
凡士林	huam se lim	Vaseline	English	Vaseline
菲林	hui lim	film	English	film
牙力	ghe lag	glass	English	glass
目头	mag tau	trademark	English	mark
抛车	pa cia	park (car)	English	park
德士	deg se	taxi	English	taxi
亚铅	a ing	iron	English	iron
五脚砌	ngou ka gih	five-foot way	Teochew+Malay	
动角	dong gag	walking stick	Malay	tongkat
榴梿	liu liêng	durian	Malay	durian
揞合(甲)	an1 gah	approximately	Malay	agak
口疑啦	ghi la	crazy	Malay	gila
油炸馃	iu za gue	fried fritters	Cantonese	
咸煎饼	ham zing bian	fried fritters	Cantonese	
拍拖	pah tua	dating	Cantonese	
拢总	long zong	everything	Old Teochew	
拢总	long zong	total	Old Teochew	
公司	gong si	share	Localised	
公司	gong si	company	Localised	
情在	ceng cai	easy-going or carelessly	Localised	
情在	ceng cai	forgive	Localised	

	Pronunciation	Meaning	Possible Sources	Source Word
色成	seg seng	bus station	English	station
鹅嘿	gho hê	go ahead	English	go ahead
郑逢	dên hong	press horn	Teochew+English	dên+horn
士茶玲	se dê lêng	steering wheel	English	steering wheel
哀林	ai lim	iodine	English	iodine
鹅突	gho dug	bottle	English	bottle
革宁	gêg lêng	indian	Malay	keling / kling
来隆	lai long	sale	Malay	lelang
乌筒	ou dang	jungle	Malay	hutan
食龟里	ziah gu1 li	employee	Teochew+English	ziah8+coolie
隆帮	long bang	care of	Malay	tumpang
红毛丹	ang mo dang	rambutan	Malay	rambutan
芒胶	mang ga	jackfruit	Malay	nangka
杜排	dou bai	squirrel	Malay	tupai
亚答	a dab	attap	Malay	attap
亚答厝	a dab cu	attap house	Malay+Teochew	attap+cu
隆沟	long gau	drain	Malay	longkang
两笼	liang lang	toilet	Malay	jambam
巴窑	ba io	wilderness	Malay	payoh
吻突	bhug dug	really	Malay	betol
儿六甲	ri lag gah	coincidence	Malay	jilaka
亚甲亚甲	a gah a gah	estimate	Malay	agak agak
妈寅	ma ing	joking, fooling around	Malay	ma-in
妈砂	ma sa	ripe	Malay	masak
财副	cai hu	book-keeper	Localised	accounts assistant
暗牌	am bai	secret agent	Localised	secret badge
白巡	bêh sung	traffic police	Localised	white inspector
钉链	deng liêng	imprison	Localised	metal chain
钉链宫	deng liêng geng	prison	Localised	metal chain institute
大人衙	dua nang ghê	Chinese protectorate	Localised	magistrate office
栈宫	zang geng	warehouse, storage	Teochew+Hokkien	storage place
丛浴宫	zang êg geng	bathroom	Hokkien	bathroom
生仔厝	sên gia cu	maternity hospital	Localised	maternity house

	Pronunciation	Meaning	Possible Sources	Source Word
食风	ziah huang	holiday	Historical	from going for a ride
食风厝	ziah huang cu	bungalow, villa	Localised	
油房	iu bang	petrol station	Localised	oil room
卜水	bog zui	soft drinks	Localised	pop drink
车	huang cia	sedan	Localised	wind vehicle
割车	guah cia	overtake while driving	Localised	
青红火	cên ang huê	traffic light	Localised	green and red light
地牛	di ghu	government inspector	Localised	
做字	zo ri	prepare legal documents	Localised	prepare paper
清丁	cêng dêng	customs officer	Localised	
罗的饼	lo di pia	biscuit	Malay+Teochew	roti+pastry
签字	ciem ri	agreement	Localised or Malay	sign paper, janji

Note: Prɔnunciations are approximated as there are variations across Teochew speakers.

Teochew Affiliated Associations

Trustee Organisations

Name	Address
Ngee Ann Kongsi (義安公司)	97 Tank Road Singapore 238066
Ban See Soon Kongsee (万世顺公司)	

Shantangs (Charity Halls)

Name	Address
Blue Cross Charitable Institution (新加坡中华善堂蓝十救济总会)	106 Pasir Panjang Road, Singapore 118534.
Seng Siang Society of the Thong Kheng Charitable Institution (同敬善堂诚善社)	14 Lor 29 Geylang, Singapore 388068.
Thong Teck Sian Tong Lian Sin Sia (同德善堂念心社)	1A Boon Teck Road, Singapore 329578.
Nam Ann Siang Theon (南安善堂)	36E Paya Lebar Crescent, Singapore 536067.
Nanyang Thong Hong Siang-Tng (南洋同奉善堂)	63 Anchorvale Walk, Singapore 545060.
Nam Hong Siang Theon (南凤善堂)	475 Yishun Ring Road, Singapore 768678.
Seu Teck Sean Tong Yiang Sin Sia (修德善堂养心社)	335 Bedok North Ave 3, Singapore 469718.
Toa Payoh Seu Teck Sean Tong (大芭窑修德善堂)	2 Lorong 5 Toa Payoh, Singapore 31937.
Poh Teck Siang-Tng (报德善堂)	109 Hougang Ave 5, Singapore 538817.
Phoh Kiu Siang-Tng (普救善堂)	15 Simon Lane, Singapore 546040.
Chung Hong Siang-Tng (新加坡崇峰善堂)	106 Pasir Panjang Road, Singapore 118534.
Cheng Hong Siang-Tng (新加坡众弘善堂)	30 Arumugam Road, Singapore 409966.

Locality Clan Associations

Area	Association	Address
Chaozhou	Teochew Poit Ip Huay Guan (潮州八邑会馆)	97 Tank Road, Singapore 238066.
Chaozhou	Singapore Teochew Federation (潮州总会)	97 Tank Road, Singapore 238066.
Chao'an	Tio Ann Third District Co-Villagers Association (潮安第三区同乡会)	618-B Geylang Road, Singapore 389557.
Chao'an	Overseas Hong Ann Villagers' Association (宏安旅外同乡会)	30 Lor 24A Geylang, Singapore 398554.
Chao'an	Teoh-Ann Leng Ho Tang Heoh Huay (潮安龙湖同乡会)	101 Upper Cross Street #03-56, Singapore 058357.
Chao'an	Teo Ann Huay Guan (潮安会馆)	48 Lor 8 Geylang, Singapore 399108.
Chao'an	Singapore Whye Teck Association (怀德联谊社)	247 South Bridge Road Singapore 058796
Chaoyang	Teo Yeonh Huai Kuan (潮阳会馆)	299 River Valley Road, Singapore 238340.
Chenghai	Chung-Lim Community Overseas Association (樟林旅外同乡会)	P.O. Box 158, Pasir Panjang Post Office, Singapore 911126.
Chenghai	Theng Hai Huay Kuan (澄海会馆)	28 Lor 25A Geylang, Singapore 388233.
Huilai	The Huilai Countrymen Association (惠来同乡会)	23B Teo Hong Road, Singapore 088332.
Jieyang	Singapore Kityang Huay Kwan (揭阳会馆)	31A & 31B Lorong 27 Geylang, Singapore 388166.
Puning	Nanyang Pho Leng Hui Kuan (南洋普宁会馆)	26 Lor 27A Geylang Singapore 388115
Raoping	Raoping Association (新加坡饶平会馆)	P.O. Box 116, Raffles City, Singapore 911704.

Kinship Clan Associations

Surname	Association	Address
刘	Low Leng Association (刘陇同乡会)	8 Lor 24 Geylang, Singapore 398491.
刘	Kityang Kwee Lim Low Clan Association (揭阳桂林刘氏公会)	15 Lor 4 Geylang, Singapore 399272.
吴	Teochew Yang Leng Lian Ngee Sia (潮州延陵联谊社)	Blk 531A Upp Cross Street #03-115, Singapore 051531.

Surname	Association	Address
孙	Sai Lin Sng Clan Association (西林孙氏同乡会)	8 Lor 27A Geylang #03-08, Singapore 388106.
张	Singapore Kim Lam Lian Ghee Sia (新加坡金銮联谊社)	134A Changi Road, Singapore 419720.
曾	Teochew Chan Clan Association (潮州曾氏公会)	No 66 Lor 24A Geylang, Singapore 398590.
李	Singapore Teochew Lee Clan Association (新加坡潮州陇西李氏公会)	39 Tessensohn Road, Singapore 217659.
杨	Singapore Teo Chew Hong Long Yeo Clan Association (新加坡潮州弘农杨氏公会)	661A Geylang Road, Singapore 389591.
杨	Teoann Sianluck Heo Yeo Clan Association Society (潮安仙乐乡杨氏同乡会)	3H Lor 12, Geylang, Singapore 398984.
林	Singapore Teo Chew Sai Ho Association (新加坡潮州西河公会)	285 River Valley Road, Singapore 238326.
林	Teo Ann Sian Tow District Lim Clan Association (潮安仙都林氏同乡会)	49 Guillemard Road, Singapore 399704.
林	The Teo-Ann District Poh Leng Village Lim Clan Association (潮安宝陇林氏同乡会)	1 North Bridge Road #03-115 High St Centre Singapore 179094
林	Sai Ho Cheo Kwa Louh Village Association (西河上官路通乡会)	618 Geylang Rd, Singapore 389557
沈	Singapore Teochew Sim Clan Association (新加坡潮州沈氏联合会)	Blk 354, Clementi Ave 2. #01-199, Singapore 120354.
蔡	Theng-Hai District Her Chiew Village Chua Clan Association (澄海渔洲蔡氏同乡会)	Blk 3017 Bedok North Street 5 #05-01, Singapore 486121.
谢	Teochew Chia Clan Association (潮州谢氏公会)	33B Guillemard Road, Singapore 399700.
郑	Kityang Tay Si Association (Singapore) (新加坡揭阳郑氏公会)	159 Tembeling Road Singapore 423668
郑	Nanyang Loy Yang Tay Clan Association (南洋礼阳郑氏同乡会)	Blk 34 Upper Cross Street #04-152, Singapore 050034.

Surname	Association	Address
郑	Khoon Kang Lian Ngee Sia (鲲江联谊社)	48 Lorong 8 Geylang, Singapore 089914.
郭	Feng Guo Fen Yang Association (凤廓汾阳公会)	21 Lor 26 Geylang, Singapore 398491.
陈	Singapore Theng Chuan Association (星洲颍川公会)	397 Upp Paya Lebar Road, Singapore 534985.
陈	Theng Chuan Ngau Thau Koo Kay Tan Clan Association (颍川鳌头旧家同乡会)	485 Sims Avenue S387557
陈	The Teo Ann Tang Hong District Tan Clan Association (潮安东凤陈氏同乡会)	42 Lor 24A Geylang, Singapore 398566.
黄	Teochew Kang Hay T'ng (潮州江夏堂)	27 Lor 24 Geylang, Singapore 398630.
黄	Huang Clan Chichang Association (黄氏炽昌联谊社)	2 Jalan Suka, Lorong 24 Geylang, Singapore 399410
成	Seng Clan Association (Singapore) (新加坡成氏宗亲会)	101 Upper Cross Street #03-56 People's Park Centre Singapore 058357.

Recreation and Culture Organizations

Name	Address
Chui Huay Lim Club (醉花林俱乐部)	190 Keng Lee Road Singapore 308409.
Hwa Siah Musical Association (华声音乐社)	86A Geylang Lorong 25A Singapore 388263.
Thau Yong Amateur Musical Association (陶融儒乐社)	68, Lorong 24A Geylang Singapore 398592.
Er Woo Amateur Musical & Dramatic Association (馀娱儒乐社)	19A/B Smith Street, Singapore 058933.
Nam Hwa Opera Limited (南华儒剧社)	28 Aliwal Street, #02-09 Aliwal Arts Centre, Singapore 199918.
The Teochew Drama Association (新加坡潮剧联谊社)	135 Rangoon Rd, Singapore 218413.

References

Sources of Photographs and Images

洪云生主编 (2002年),《新加坡潮州文化展特刊》, 新加坡: 新加坡潮州八邑会馆. (Page 63)

黄赞发、陈桂源 (2008年),《潮汕华侨历史文化图录》, 山东美术出版社出版. (Page 21 *bottom right*, 22 *top left*)

李炳炎. (Page 114 *bottom right*, 141 *top right*, 142, 145 *top left*)

李志贤 (2011年),《流金岁月：醉花林俱乐部一六六周年暨新会所开幕双庆纪念特辑》, 新加坡: 醉花林俱乐部. (Page 41, 62 *top right*¸ 76 *bottom right*)

林朝虹、林伦伦编著 (2012年),《全本潮汕方言歌谣评注》, 广州: 花城出版社 (Page 30 *bottom*)

林凯龙 (2017年),《潮汕古俗: 四海潮人的精神家园》, 香港: 香港中和出版. (Page 105 *top left* and *top right*, 107 *bottom right*)

潘醒农 (1950年),《马来亚潮侨通鉴》, 新加坡: 南岛出版社. (Page 77 *top right*)

潘醒农主编 (1979年),《新加坡潮州八邑会馆金禧纪念刊》, 新加坡：新加坡潮州八邑会馆. (Page 77 *bottom right*)

姚梦桐 (2017年),《流动迁移在地经历——新加坡视觉艺术现象(1886-1945)》, (Page 90 *top right*)

张美生 (2011年).《潮汕侨批赏析》, 香港: 天马出版有限公司. (Page 60)

郑国浩主编 (2008年),《潮州古建筑》, 中国建筑工业出版社. (Page 25 *bottom left*, *right*)

《擎青学校五十周年纪念刊》(1997年). Singapore: Kheng Cheng School. (Page 69)

《新加坡潮州八邑会馆成立七十周年纪念》(2000年), 新加坡：新加坡潮州八邑会馆. (Page 79 *bottom*)

《潮涌: 新加坡潮州八邑会馆八十週年纪念特刊》(2009年), 新加坡：新加坡潮州八邑会馆. (Page 79 *top*, 80 *top right*)

BELS Collection, courtesy of National Archives of Singapore. (Page 122)

Boden-Kloss Collection, courtesy of National Archives of Singapore. (Page 56)

C.K. Tang (1993). *Out of the Tin Trunk : An In-House Publication of C.K. Tang Ltd*. Singapore : C.K. Tang Ltd. (Page 145 *bottom left*)

Chew Yew Lih, Heng Chye Kiang, Gretchiu Liu (2003). *The House of Tan Yeok Nee: The Conservation of a National Monument*. Winpeak Investment Pte Limited & Wingem Investment Pte Limited. (Page 121 *top*)

Chui Huay Lim Club. (Page 76)

Gretchen Liu Collection, courtesy of National Archives of Singapore. (Page 53 *top left*)

Gretchen Liu (1999). Singapore: *A Pictorial History, 1819–2000*. Singapore: Didier Millet and National Heritage Board. (Page 123 *bottom right*)

Koh Nguang How. (Page 93, *bottom*)

Lee Kip Lin Collection. Courtesy of the National Library Board, Singapore. (Page 131)

Lim Chong Hsien Collection, courtesy of National Archives of Singapore. (Page 53 *top right*)

Provided by Margaret Leng Tan. (Page 87 *bottom left*)

Ministry of Culture Collection, courtesy of National Archives of Singapore. (Page 48)

Ministry of Information and the Arts Collection, courtesy of National Archives of Singapore (page 66, 115)

Nanyang Thong Hong Siang-Tng. (Page 82 *top right*)

National Archives of Singapore. (Page 54, 58 *top right*, 61, 76 *bottom right*)

National Museum of Singapore. (Page 42-43)

National University Press. (Page 57 *top left*)

Ngee Ann Kongsi (Page 68 *top left*, 71 *bottom left*)

People's Association. (Page 139)

Ronni Pinsler Collection, courtesy of National Archives of Singapore. (Page 37, 57 *bottom right*, 118, 119, 132, 137)

RSP Architects Planners & Engineers. (Page 121 *bottom right*, 125 *bottom*)

Salvation Army of Singapore. (Page 124 *bottom right*)

Singapore Teochew Poit Ip Huay Kuan. (Page 80 *bottom left*)

Steven Seng. (Page 100, 138)

Sumiko Tan. (2005). *Ngee Ann Kongsi: Into The Next Millennium*. Singapore: Ngee Ann Kongsi. (Page 74 *bottom left*, 75 *top left*)

Terence Tan. (Page 38)

Teo Yeonh Huai Kuan (Page 68 *bottom right*)

The 1602 world map, Kunyu Wanguo Quantu, is owned by the James Ford Bell Trust. It has been loaned to the University of Minnesota for the benefit of the James Ford Bell Library. (Page 33)

Tuan Meng High School Alumni Association. (Page 65)

Urban Redevelopment Authority Collection, courtesy of National Archives of Singapore. (Page 71)

Xinghua Primary School. Retrieved from http://xinghuapri.moe.edu.sg/school-information/school-history 3 Jan 2018. (Page 69 *top right*)

Publications

蔡海松 (2012年)，《潮汕民居》，广州：暨南大学出版社

曾楚楠、叶汉钟 (2011年),《潮州工夫茶话》，广州：暨南大学出版社

陈达 (1938年),《南洋华侨与闽粤社会》, 长沙：商务印书馆

陈泽泓 (2013年),《潮汕文化概说》第 2 版, 广州：广东人民出版社

陈骅 (2003年),《潮人在新加坡》, 香港：公元出版社

林凯龙 (2013年)，《潮汕老厝：四海潮人的心灵故乡》，北京：生活·读书·新知三联书店

林伦轮、吴勤生主编 (2001年),《潮汕文化大观》, 广州：花城出版社

林伦伦(1997年),《潮汕方言与普通话》, 汕头: 汕头大学出版社

林伦伦 (2012年),《潮汕方言：潮人的精神家园》, 广州：暨南大学出版社

郭马凤、魏影秋 (2011年)，《潮汕美术陶瓷与刺绣抽纱》，香港：天马出版有限公司

洪云生主编 (2002年),《新加坡潮州文化展特刊》, 新加坡：新加坡潮州八邑会馆

黄枝连，<新加坡华人布匹业>, 载 (2014年)《南洋大学新加坡华族行业史调查研究报告》, 新加坡：八方文化创作室

黄挺、陈占山 (2001年),《潮汕史上册》, 广州：广东人民出版社

黄挺 (1997年),《潮汕文化源流》, 广州：广东高等教育出版社

赖素春, <反殖时代新加坡戏曲的再度繁荣(1945-1965)>, 载周宁主编 (2007年),《东南亚华语戏剧史》, 厦门大学出版社

李炳炎 (2014年),《枫溪潮州窑 (1860-1956)》, 广州：暨南美术出版社

李炳炎 (2015年),《潮瓷下南洋》, 深圳报业集团出版社

李谷僧、端蒙中学 (1956年)，《新加坡端蒙中学五十周年纪念刊》，新加坡：新加坡端蒙中学

李志贤, <新加坡潮人善堂溯源—兼论其在早期移民社会的建构基础>，摘自 (2005年),《第五届潮学国际研讨会论文集》, 香港：公元出版有限公司

李志贤 (2005年),《从宗教仪式看新加坡潮人善堂信仰的文化内涵》, ScholarBank@NUS Repository

李志贤编 (2003年),《海外潮人的移民经验》, 新加坡：新加坡潮州八邑会馆

李志贤 (2011年),《流金岁月：醉花林俱乐部一六六周年暨新会所开幕双庆纪念特辑》, 新加坡：醉花林俱乐部

梁启超 (1937年), <中国殖民八大伟人传>, 载《饮冰室合集·专集》(第三册), 中华书局

潘醒侬等编纂 (1932年)，《新加坡指南》, 新加坡：南洋出版社

潘醒农 (1950年)，《马来亚潮侨通鉴》，新加坡：南岛出版社

潘醒农主编 (1979年),《新加坡潮州八邑会馆金禧纪念刊》，新加坡：新加坡潮州八邑会馆.

<马来亚丛谈之廿四陈天蔡地佘皇帝许云樵教授撰·新加坡电台播>,《南洋商报》(1961年2月2日)

<南来约有七十年歷史最初抵星為老玉楼春夜戏多演小生花旦戏纸影乃在白字戏之后>,《南洋商报》(1963年4月2日)

<政府放宽街头演戏禁令批准白昼演出时间自上午十时至下午七时止唯以不妨碍治安为前提>,《南洋商报》(1964年8月9日)

<六处申请演街头戏昨日未获警方批准梨园公会吁酌量情形准予演出需要时可缩短时间或派警保护>,《南洋商报》(1964年8月15日)

<新天彩潮剧团明晚开锣义演三看刘金定及挡马收入捐作国家剧场基金>,《南洋商报》(1967年6月19日)

<万世顺公司决定明年起发给端蒙中学生助学金端蒙中学现有申请表格>,《南洋商报》(1967年9月11日)

<义安工艺学院昨晚举行隆重移交典礼义安公司再捐献三十万元以供建校用途教育部长保証政府将尽力支持>,《南洋商报》(1968年9月20日)

<四海通银行与华侨银行即将携手合作扩大金融业务股票交换为三股对一股>,《南洋商报》(1972年12月16日)

<最古老的潮剧院怡园和哲园>,《联合晚报》(1983年4月12日)

<配合国家的教育趋势，完成新的使命－公立擎青学校>,《联合晚报》(1985年1月22日)

<庆维新、庆升平、怡园、哲园...早期地方戏戏院今何在？>,《联合早报》(1987年2月8日)

<华南学校和潮闽两帮派的关系>,《联合早报》(1987年4月5日)

<财启村怀古>,《联合晚报》(1987年4月6日)

<培英学校风雨68年>,《联合晚报》(1987年5月24日)

<《丽的》16位广播员首次合作灌录歌唱专辑>,《联合晚报》(1987年7月11日)

<"港脚"的兴衰>,《联合晚报》(1987年7月23日)

<木偶戏兴衰>,《联合早报》(1988年10月2日)

<木炭有荣史·传薪潮阳人>,《联合早报》(1988年12月11日)

<作育英才潮州人的不朽事业>,《联合早报》(1989年10月1日)

<潮人陶瓷业鼎盛岁月>,《联合早报》(2002年6月24日)

<崇峰善堂发度岁金给300老人>,《联合晚报》(2009年1月13日)

<大批珍贵书画捐赠后极少展出陈之初之子陈玉仪：太可惜>,《联合早报》(2016年5月17日)

<新加坡潮州总会修改章程可直接邀潮人翘楚任领导>,《联合早报》(2016年7月3日)

沈敦武，<不应被遗忘的东兴汇路>,《中国邮政报》(第2308期 2015年8月26日 星期三)

陈镇景，<浅谈潮州方言>，《潮州日报》(2014年10月9日)

张豪禧、沈象仁，<潮州方言：语言文化中的"古汉语活化石>，《潮州日报》(2013年3月28日)

Singapore Duty Question. *The Singapore Free Press and Mercantile Advertiser* (17 December 1835), Page 2

Singapore Municipal Committee. *The Straits Times* (15 May 1855), Page 5

Report Of The Commission Upon The Condition Of Chinese Labourers, And Their Immigration. *Straits Observer (Singapore)* (11 November 1876)

The Riots. *The Straits Times* (23 December 1876), Page 2

Straits Times Weekly Issue (14 June 1883), Page 6

Handbook Of The Swatow Vernacular, *Straits Times Weekly Issue* (6 May 1886), Page 8

The Labour Commission, *Straits Times Weekly Issue* (29 October 1890), Page 1.

Yeo Kian Guan Appellant. *The Straits Times* (10 April 1891), Page 2

The Chinese Consul General. *The Straits Times* (16 February 1895), Page 3

Regulations for the Guidance of Chinese Advisory Board, Singapore. *The Straits Times* (23 December 1889), Page 3

The Treaty Port Of Swatow, *Eastern Daily Mail And Straits Morning Advertiser* (27 December 1906), Page 6

Committee: St. Mary's Home., *The Singapore Free Press And Mercantile Advertiser* (1 June 1907), Page 7

Longevity in Litigation. *The Straits Times* (14 December 1922), Page 10

Chinese Benefactor Of 1845. *The Straits Times* (24 September 1932), Page 12

Ngee Ann Kongsi. Malaya Tribune (27 September 1932), Page 14

Closing From St. Mary's Home., *Malaya Tribune* (19 November 1932), Page 14

Chinese Topics In Malaya, *The Straits Times* (16 October 1934), Page 13

Child Actors. *The Straits Times* (5 April 1935), Page 10

Temple House To Be Headquarters Of Salvation Army, *The Singapore Free Press And Mercantile Advertiser* (15 January 1938), Page 9

Town Hall For Chinese, *The Straits Times* (11 February 1939), Page 12

War Delays Building, *The Straits Times* (29 October 1939), Page 7.

Chinese Charitable Union Gets To Work Bureau Formed. *Syonan Shimbun* (23 January 1945)

New Colony Bank Opens Next Year, *The Straits Times* (16 Oct 1948)

Colony Amateur Musicians, *The Straits Times* (20 January 1949), Page 4

Children's Law In Force Soon, *The Singapore Free Press* (20 July 1950), Page 5

'Army' To Restore 'Temple House', *The Straits Times* (25 September 1950), Page 7

Governor Opens 'Army' Hq, *The Straits Times* (7 July 1951), Page 5

1,200-Pupil Limit: 'Big Three' Back Govt. School Plan, *The Straits Times* (11 January 1957), Page 5

'Go Ahead' For $1.5m Chamber Building (*The Singapore Free Press*, 6 June 1961), Page 1

Mystery date? The facts. *The Straits Times* (8 October 1964), Page 10

OCBC—Conservative Yet Progressive, *The Straits Times* (3 September 1974), Page 11

New School Building, *The Straits Times* (12 July 1975), Page 17

Banker Sets Up Fund For Charity. *The Straits Times* (15 April 1980), Page 9

Sailing Down The River Of Old, *The Straits Times* (10 August 1982), Page 1.

Remittances To China Kin Drop As Emigrants Here Age, *The Straits Times* (14 June 1987), Page 14

Salvation Army Hq Sold To Cockpit For $20m, *The Straits Times* (20 April 1991), Page 20

Wing Tai-Led Group Pays $380m For Cockpit Site, *The Business Times* (27 September 1996), Page 1

Restoration To Cost $12 Million, *The Straits Times* (26 January 1999), Page 28

Late philanthropist's children donate $10 million in his name. *TODAY* (25 June 2001), Page 2

Searching For Loved Ones, *The Straits Times* (1 April 2002), Page 4

Giving back. *TODAY* (16 April 2002), Page 4

Paya Lebar's 'Secret $1 Clinic' Relocated To Hougang , *TODAY* (2 August 2005), Page 7

Wing Tai Associate Sells Heritage House Office Tower, *The Straits Times* (23 Jan 2007), Page 44

More Needy Seniors Signing Up For Free Funeral Services. *Today* (18 December 2016)

Online Sources

汕头市政府门户网站, http://www.shantou.gov.cn/cnst/jbxzqh/zjst_lmtt.shtml

中国潮州政府网站 - 潮州市人民政府, http://www.chaozhou.gov.cn/sqgm/index.jhtml

揭阳市人民政府门户网站 , http://www.jieyang.gov.cn/List.aspx?q_cid=47

<新加坡广东会馆简史>, http://www.sfcca.sg/en/kwangtung

黄挺、杜经国《潮汕地区人口的发展(唐--元)》https://wenku.baidu.com/view/8823b64bcf84b9d528ea7a3e.html

黄挺、杜经国《潮汕地区人口的发展(明)》https://wenku.baidu.com/view/5525e5da50e2524de5187e3e.html

Department of Statistics Singapore. Retrieved from: http://www.singstat.gov.sg/about-us/history#sthash.CAwe5XeQ.dpuf

Lien Foundation. Retrieved from: http://www.lienfoundation.org/affiliates

Ngee Ann Secondary School. Retrieved from: http://ngeeannsec.moe.edu.sg/about-us/background

Singapore Fish Merchants General Association. Retrieved from: http://www.fishmerchant.org.sg/about.htm

Teochew Rythms By Thau Yong Amateur Musical Association. Retrieved from: http://scarlet.c3a.org.sg/activity/teochew-rythms-glv

US Department of State. *The Opening to China Part II: the Second Opium War, the United States, and the Treaty of Tianjin, 1857-1859*. Retrieved from: https://2001-2009.state.gov/r/pa/ho/time/dwe/82012.htm

Archives

Report by the Commissioner appointed to enquire into the State of Labour in the Straits Settlements and the Protected Native States (1891). National Archives of Singapore

1891 Report on the Census of the Straits Settlements

Tay Lee Huat 郑利发 (5 Mar 1988). Interview by Tan Bee Luan [Tape recording]. *Vanishing Trades.* Accession Number 000816, Oral History Centre.

Phua Tong Gek 潘中玉 (23 Sep 1987). Interview by Jesley Chua Chee Huan [Tape recording]. *Vanishing Trades*. Accession Number 000893, Oral History Centre.